THE COMMON THREAD

KEVIN J. MORONEY

The
LITURGY
Common
LOOKING
Thread
FORWARD

CHURCH
PUBLISHING
INCORPORATED

Church Publishing
19 East 34th Street
New York, NY 10016
www.churchpublishing.org

Cover design by Jennifer Kopec, 2Pug Design
Typeset by Denise Hoff

Library of Congress Cataloging-in-Publication Data

Names: Moroney, Kevin J., author.
Title: The common thread : liturgy looking forward / Kevin J. Moroney.
Identifiers: LCCN 2020046829 (print) | LCCN 2020046830 (ebook) | ISBN 9781640653672 (paperback) | ISBN 9781640653689 (epub)
Subjects: LCSH: Liturgical reform. | Episcopal Church--History--21st century.
Classification: LCC BX5940 .M675 2021 (print) | LCC BX5940 (ebook) | DDC 264/.03--dc23
LC record available at https://lccn.loc.gov/2020046829
LC ebook record available at https://lccn.loc.gov/2020046830

For Elsa and Maggie, my beloved daughters—
Remember that redemption is always near.

Love forever,
Daddy

Contents

CHAPTER ONE

Starting the Conversation

WHY DO YOU go to church? Let me guess. You were raised in a denomination of some European background; dropped out immediately after confirmation; had an emotional crisis during your late teens when a friend fell off a cliff and died as part of an overnight drinking party; went to the funeral and sat in the church realizing that an important part of your life was being neglected; then after a year of soul searching, had a "come to Jesus" moment that set the course for your entire adult life.

It's complicated. First of all, that's not your story; it's mine. I believe you have a story that is just as important to you or why else would you be here? There are as many answers to that opening question as there are stars in the sky; they all get underneath our skin and make us tear up from time to time. I still miss Dave and I still pray for him every time we pray for the deceased because I know I wouldn't be here without him. Yet none of this—the struggles, the stars in the sky—is unique to church people. The same can be said of those who chose not to stay in the Church, as well as for those whose life began or continued with a different narrative. So let's forget the triumphal stuff. It's all complicated and human and meaningful but I can't write for everybody. This book is for those of us who have decided to stick it out in the Church and, to a certain degree, in the Episcopal Church. That, too, is complicated but we have our reasons. For me, one of those reasons is that I love Christian worship; particularly the Roman Catholic, Pentecostal, and Episcopal/Anglican worship that have made me who I am. I love it all so much that I wanted to teach it for a living, and God has mercifully allowed me to do just that. Oh, and I love God and by God I mean the Trinity. I should have said that first because, you know, now that I haven't, the angry God of my childhood might slay me, and rightly so.

Yes, I am an Episcopal priest, but before that, I am a Christian and before that, I am a human. I started as a Bible guy, but went to a seminary where chapel was the center of life and praying with the community every day, twice a day (except when rebelling), paved the way for biblical passion to lead to liturgical passion. I feel like a better version of myself when worshipping. I enjoy pattern and ritual and well synchronized movements that mean things. I have a funny feeling that you may, as well.

So a Jersey boy who thinks about liturgy and prays about liturgy and teaches liturgy is one of the people optimistic about this new era of liturgical renewal in the Episcopal Church. I not only believe that we can do this, but I believe that the whole Episcopal family can stay together and maybe, maybe, *maybe* even get a little stronger for doing so—and that is why I am writing this book. I didn't say it would help us get bigger. I worry about that, too, but I have no ideas. I do have an idea about how we can shape liturgical renewal but I am going to take a bit of a slow road to get to that idea so I can explain what it is and why it might be a good one. Leave nothing behind. Every crumb is sacred. Then I'm going to retire. I get tired more easily now.

Why do you attend the church you do? It takes a lot of courage to visit a new church, even if you are lucky enough to know someone who already worships there. Or, maybe you are the faithful remnant who still attends the church of your childhood. God knows we could use more of you. I have no idea where all the Episcopalians have gone. It's like they evaporated with the polar ice caps. Most parishes I have known consist of former Roman Catholics or former Evangelicals or former something else, which means that most of us had that experience of timorously entering the previously unknown church building. If you did go through the unique agony of visiting a new church you first had to get there, and if you were driving, you had to find a place to park. Once parked, you had to find the door that everyone *actually* uses; once inside you were either greeted or not by someone who was either friendly or not (I've been doing this stuff for years; I know). Then your brain went into processing overload. You either did or did not resonate with the space (normal is what we know). You either did or did not receive helpful information on how to follow the service. The worship space was either full, empty, or somewhere in between and you either felt comfortable or uncomfortable with how many people were there. And you got an early impression of whether or not there was anyone else there who was remotely like you. And then, after all that, the service started.

And now here we are. What keeps you there? I have to believe that one thing you and I share in common is a love for the worship of God. I am not saying that worship is the most important thing we do, but I have been a priest long enough to know that any Spirit-driven energy a church has draws from what happens when we're together on Sunday morning, and that is primarily for worship. It's important. It's meaningful. The only problem is that like every other important thing in our life it keeps changing.

For the last decade and a half, I have been a priest of the Episcopal Diocese of Pennsylvania. There's a lot of New Jersey in me but that will come in later. On Saturday, November 7, 2015, the above-mentioned diocese sat patiently through the report of their delegates to the General Convention of the Episcopal Church that had taken place earlier in the year. I confess that, for me, events like diocesan conventions are a kind of church equivalent to medieval dental practices: we just sit still while all the hope is painfully yanked out of us. I do know many people who work very hard to prove me wrong about that. God bless them—I'm too far gone. The report on the approval of rites for same-sex marriage came and went without noticeable reaction. What's so earth-shattering about that? A description of the proposed restructuring of the national church passed by with a similar non-response from the four hundred or so gathered. Yawn and check the time. However, when the presenter noted that a resolution had passed that could lead to a revision of the Book of Common Prayer, the people who filled that cathedral spontaneously, audibly, and unmistakably *groaned*. I can suggest with reasonable confidence that the involuntary expression of primordial angst was a response to either the memory of the introduction of the 1979 prayer book, a reaction to the sense that the Episcopal Church was just beginning to emerge from what felt like a long period of church-wide conflict and didn't need any more, or both.

The end of the Church's exclusive claim on Sundays. The ordination of women. Prayer book revision. Rising divorce rates. Growing secularism. Changing views on human sexuality. Changing definitions of what constitutes a family. The ordination of those in the LGBTQ community. The slowness of institutional change. The resistance of the institution to actually changing. The passage of progressive sounding resolutions as a substitute for actually changing. The death of the World War II generation. The catastrophic drop in church attendance as a result of the death of the World War II generation. That, coupled with what some see as the decline of Anglo culture. That, coupled with the fact that the Episcopal

Church is still overwhelmingly Anglo and does not seem particularly motivated to become anything else. The fear of our extinction as a church.

It's exhausting; can we just take a break? Do we really need a new prayer book? If we are to revise, who is going to make the decisions about our worship? How do we know that the theology of the Trinity enshrined in the creeds and prayers of the 1979 prayer book will be preserved in a new book? Will tree hugging ceremonies be placed in the same volume as Holy Baptism and Holy Eucharist (yes, I have heard this question more than once)? The issue that hovers over all of these questions, over this book and everything it includes (or not), is the issue of power. God is power, language is power, the General Convention is power, and the power to change our language about God is an alarming level of power. This issue will return frequently, but let's tuck it in for now, take a breath, and keep going.

Technically, what was approved at the 2015 General Convention was a resolution for the Standing Commission on Liturgy and Music (SCLM) to "prepare a plan for the comprehensive revision of the current Book of Common Prayer." Our General Convention only meets every three years and a prayer book must be approved by two successive conventions, thus it would take a minimum of three conventions to produce a new prayer book, which would require the miracle of producing all revision work between 2018 and 2021 in order to approve a new prayer book by 2024. Couldn't happen that fast.

Nonetheless, it should come as no surprise that, as delegates to the 79th General Convention of the Episcopal

Church prepared to gather in Austin, Texas, in the summer of 2018, participants packed their bags knowing that one of the big topics coming before the convention was whether or not to revise the 1979 Book of Common Prayer.[1] The SCLM presented two options to the 2018 General Convention:

> Option One . . . envisions a decision by the upcoming General Convention to move into the revision process immediately, the first stage being to gather data, resources, and ideas, and then set up the structure to begin drafting immediately after 2021 General Convention. Option Two . . . envisions a slower pace, while remaining open to Prayer Book revision in the future. Option Two invites the whole church to broaden its familiarity with the 1979 Prayer Book and the history that underlies it, and provides for time to reflect as a body on the significance of common prayer in our tradition.[2]

The House of Deputies passed Option One, but the House of Bishops replaced it with a much longer and more complex resolution that intends to set the direction of liturgical revision in the Episcopal Church for years to

---

1 The General Convention is made up of the House of Bishops and the House of Deputies, which includes both laity and clergy other than bishops. General Convention meets every three years.

2 2018 Blue Book, 194, https://extranet.generalconvention.org/staff/files/download/21368.

come.[3] The resolution itself is a study in Anglican theological method: there is a clear attempt to be comprehensive and inclusive of all traditions and perspectives within the Episcopal Church by providing language that speaks to every group, but in doing so it generates a distinctly Anglican kind of ambiguity that requires interpretive negotiation between the words.

Resolution A068 reads as follows:

1. *Resolved,* That the 79th General Convention, pursuant to Article X of the Constitution, authorize the ongoing work of liturgical and Prayer Book revision for the future of God's mission through the Episcopal branch of the Jesus movement. And, that it do so upon the core theological work of loving, liberating, life-giving reconciliation and creation care; and be it further

2. *Resolved,* that our methodology be one of a dynamic process for discerning common worship, engaging all the baptized, while practicing accountability to The Episcopal Church; and be it further

3. *Resolved,* That the 79th General Convention create a Task Force on Liturgical

---

3   The full resolution can be found online at The Archives of the Episcopal Church, The Acts of Convention, 2018-A068, https://www.episcopalarchives.org/cgi-bin/acts/acts_resolution.pl?resolution=2018-A068.

and Prayer Book Revision (TFLPBR), the membership of which will be jointly appointed by the Presiding Bishop and the President of the House of Deputies, and will report to the appropriate legislative(s) of the 80th General Convention, ensuring that diverse voices of our church are active participants in this liturgical revision by constituting a group with leaders who represent the expertise, gender, age, theology, regional, and ethnic diversity of the church, to include, 10 laity, 10 priests or deacons, and 10 Bishops; and be it further

4. *Resolved,* That this Convention memorialize the 1979 Book of Common Prayer as a Prayer Book of the church preserving the psalter, liturgies, The Lambeth Quadrilateral, Historic Documents, and Trinitarian Formularies ensuring its continued use; and be it further

5. *Resolved,* That this church continue to engage the deep Baptismal and Eucharistic theology and practice of the 1979 Prayer Book; and be it further

6. *Resolved,* That bishops engage worshiping communities in experimentation and the creation of alternative texts to offer to the wider church, and that each

diocese be urged to create a liturgical commission to collect, reflect, teach and share these resources with the TFLPBR; and be it further

7. *Resolved,* That the TFLPBR in consultation with the Standing Commission on Structure, Governance, Constitution and Canons is directed to propose to the 80th General Convention revisions to the Constitution and Canons to enable The Episcopal Church to be adaptive in its engagement of future generations of Episcopalians, multiplying, connecting, and disseminating new liturgies for mission, attending to prayer book revision in other provinces of the Anglican Communion; and be it further

8. *Resolved,* That liturgical and Prayer Book revision will continue in faithful adherence to the historic rites of the Church Universal as they have been received and interpreted within the Anglican tradition of 1979 Book of Common Prayer, mindful of our existing ecumenical commitments, while also providing space for, encouraging the submission of, and facilitating the perfection of rites that will arise from the continual movement of the Holy Spirit among us and growing insights of our Church; and be it further

9. *Resolved,* That such revision utilize the riches of Holy Scripture and our Church's liturgical, cultural, racial, generational, linguistic, gender, physical ability, class and ethnic diversity in order to share common worship; and be it further

10. *Resolved,* That our liturgical revision utilize inclusive and expansive language and imagery for humanity and divinity; and be it further

11. *Resolved,* That our liturgical revision shall incorporate and express understanding, appreciation, and care of God's creation; and be it further

12. *Resolved,* That our liturgical revision take into consideration the use of emerging technologies which provide access to a broad range of liturgical resources; and be it further

13. *Resolved,* That the SCLM create a professional dynamic equivalence translation of The Book of Common Prayer 1979 and the Enriching Our Worship Series in Spanish, French, and Haitian Creole; and that the SCLM diversify the publication formats of new resources, liturgies and rites to include online publishing; and be it further

14. *Resolved,* That this church ensure that, at each step of the revision process, all materials be professionally translated into English, Spanish, French, and Haitian Creole, following the principles of dynamic equivalence and that no new rites or liturgical resources be approved by this church until such translations are secured; and be it further

15. *Resolved,* That the TFLPBR shall report to the 80th General Convention; and be it further

16. *Resolved,* That there being $201,000 in the proposed budget for the translation of liturgical materials, that the Executive Council be encouraged to identify additional funds in the amount of $200,000 to begin this liturgical revision.

What on earth does all that mean? It is, err, a bit circular in its progression. At a minimum, it must mean that the 1979 prayer book will continue in some fashion and be the basis for revision work, and that we will address those things which our current prayer book left undone in regards to inclusive and expansive language, creation theology, and drawing on the diverse cultures of the Episcopal Church, with some provision for approving new liturgies more quickly. With that said, there is nothing in the resolution about how long the 1979 Prayer Book will remain in use or what the final result of this

new era of revision is going to look like. The resolution
sets the direction without limiting possibilities. That task
has been left to the task force to figure out.

Wait, I have an email in my inbox. I have been
appointed to serve on this task force. How did that
happen? Actually, it's an honor to be asked to help and
I am proud to do so. All snarkiness aside, the Episcopal
Church has been very good to me for more than thirty
years and I wouldn't recognize my life without it. I now
have an opportunity to make a contribution to the life of
this church that has given me such a good life and I pray
to God that I don't blow it.

While the creation of the task force in clause 3 is signif-
icant because much of the work related to the resolution
will be done by its members, a far more radical statement is made in clause 2 of the resolution, calling this
new era "a dynamic process for discerning common worship, engaging all the baptized. . . ." Generally speaking,
liturgical revision has always been the work of liturgical
specialists and church leaders, who then pass their work
through the consideration of the General Convention
and on to dioceses and congregations. By calling for the
engagement of all the baptized, this resolution clearly
envisions the involvement of every order of ministry (lay
persons, bishops, priests and deacons, BCP 855) at the
level of liturgical creation, and that is new, and that is all
of us!

So this book is an attempt to have a conversation about
who we are as Christians, why we do what we do in worship (on a good day), what we can do now, and how we
can do it, written by someone who has been doing this

work for quite some time and who sees an opportunity to demonstrate to ourselves that we can move forward liturgically without falling into another soul-wrenching conflict that sends more people running for the door. Yes, we can.

CHAPTER TWO

A Couple of Words about Couples of Words

I WAS A DOCTORAL student in Dublin, Ireland, and one of the joys and challenges of doing doctoral research is the volume of reading that has to be done. Some of it was life changing and some of it made me want to jump out the window. Staying with the first category, two liturgical scholars who had an impact on me were Lutherans Gail Ramshaw and Gordon Lathrop. Gail writes on liturgical language, particularly on ways we can expand the range of possibilities for our language about God, and this has stayed with me. Gordon holds the world record for frequent use of the word "juxtaposition." If you doubt me on this point just read his book *Holy Things: A Liturgical Theology*. He sees meaning as often being generated by the tension between two ideas working "in juxtaposition" with one another. Old and New. Word and Sacrament. Baptism and Eucharist. I liked the way they thought and wrote, so imagine my joy when I moved back from Dublin, found myself in the Philadelphia region where I started hanging out at the library of the Lutheran Theological Seminary, and learned that they are not only a couple of great liturgical theologians, they are a great couple; they are married! During those years they were kind enough to befriend and mentor me and I will forever be in their debt. Additionally, their work along with countless others on *Evangelical Lutheran Worship*, published in 2006, should be something that Episcopalians look at when considering our own new liturgical creations.

So with Gail and Gordon providing some inspiration, I want to say a couple of words about couples of words. Four couplets to be precise. I realize that there is a danger in appearing to imply that the world can be reduced to binary forms. Shades of truth abound. I am only agreeing that there is some truth to be found this way, and liturgical truth in particular. The first couplet will provide a point of clarification, the second will lead us into the minefield of liturgical language about God, the third will suggest a point of tense balance that all liturgy needs, and the fourth represents my broad conceptual liturgical understanding. I recall my friend and colleague from Dublin, Andrew Pierce, saying that studying theology is about becoming confused at a more informed level. Love that, so let's get the confusion going at a slightly deeper level.

The first couplet is "liturgy" and "worship." The need for clarifying these terms is that, in my experience, there are those who tend to use the first and there are those who tend to use the second, and for historically complicated reasons. The term "liturgy" is generally the preference for traditional or more academically oriented Christians, and the term "worship" the preference for those who place value on using popular cultural practices and infusing them with the substance of the Christian faith. Jeanne Halgren Kilde demonstrated in her book *When the Church Became Theatre* that the distinction really took off in the nineteenth century, with eighteenth century roots. An excellent read. The outdoor revivals of the Great Awakening led to indoor revivalist churches of the nineteenth century, with liturgical historian James White providing us with the language of a formalist and informalist split. I prefer the language of ritualist and revivalist but that may betray my catholic sympathies. Oh, how we bicker over words! Ever since those days of the Great Awakening, the two groups generally did not trust each other. There were "concerns" if not outright condemnations coming from both directions. Liturgical churches were and are thought to be dead, focusing on the "vain repetitions of [people]." Worship churches were and are accused of being concerned with personal religious entertainment; they have no historical or theological depth but put on a great, or at least big, show.

I mentioned earlier that I was a biblicist before I was a liturgist, which is why I know a fair bit about that fabled war. I learned the Bible by studying the biblical languages with Pentecostals; I find it useful to begin by exploring what words meant originally and in scripture. The term "liturgy" is popularly mistranslated as meaning "the work of the people." It is a great idea that the liturgy is where all the baptized work together to sing and speak and proclaim the love of God we know in Jesus Christ. A great idea, but not really what that word has ever meant. It comes from a Greek word *leiturgia*, which was used in classical Greek to refer to the building of roads and bridges for the public good by people of means, sometimes using a fair bit of leverage. It was an early kind of taxation and application. It entered scripture when those who translated the Hebrew Bible into Greek thought it was a handy term for describing the work of the priests in the temple. They were performing *leiturgia*, good works done for the benefit of other people. It actually doesn't show up much in the Christian Testament but is used, for example, to describe the financial gift Paul was raising for the saints back in Jerusalem. It really came back after Constantine made peace with the Church in the fourth century, which is when Christians were given bright new shiny basilicas, that is, Roman civic buildings, for their liturgies, in which they did good work for the benefit of the people. It may very well be that the newer version, the work of the people, will continue to catch on so much that the word actually changes meaning. Words do change meaning based on use. I just want to make the point that that is not where it comes from. Academically, I tend to use the word liturgy to describe all the things that make up the practice of shared worship: the space, art, music, prayer texts, proclamation, and people that weave something remarkable together when Christians meet. I like knitting language. I probably got it from Gail but I can't be sure.

Worship also has an interesting background and has only become an exclusively religious term relatively recently. It comes from the old English *worthshippe*, and has to do with placing a great value on something. In all the English prayer books from 1549 to 1662 the term "worship" was used to refer, not to God, but for something a fair bit more arousing. The groom said to the bride, "With this ring I thee wed, with my body I thee worship." As I said, words do change meaning and now the word is used in the exclusive domain of the Divine. For the purposes of this book I will use the terms "liturgy" and "worship" synonymously, because it is hard to use the same word over and over and over again, and they provide a kind of balance to one another.

The second couplet is "God" and "Father." This, it seems to me, is the starting point for any discussion about inclusive and expansive language. Practicing inclusive language means using gender neutral words when a gender is not indicated, that is, masculine forms do not represent the whole. Practicing expansive language involves using a wide range of words for God rather than settling dogmatically on the masculine ones. The Bible has a variety of language for God. The prayer book has a clear preference for one term: Father. A common way many of us deal with inclusive language as it relates to Deity is to substitute the word "God" every time the prayer book says "Father." It removes the masculine term and substitutes it with a gender-neutral one. The same is often done with male pronouns. In 2018, General Convention passed Resolution D078 which, for the most part, does just that but confusingly calls it expansive language when it is really inclusive language. Again, words. The first thing I want to say is that language is imperfect and God is ineffable (see the collect for All Saints' Day, BCP 194, 245), so any attempt to fix one problem often creates another. We better get used to that. The choice to replace Father with God is usually a principled call for linguistic justice for those who have been taught indirectly and incorrectly, but nonetheless clearly, by representatives of a male-dominated power structure that our Deity is male and that if using God is an imperfect substitute for Father, then it may be no more imperfect than the constant hammering of the male nail as language for God. That call for linguistic justice has my full support. With that said, as we move forward on liturgical revision and make more intentional choices about our God language, expansive language principles can help us to draw more on the riches of scripture and tradition to put "Father" in juxtaposition with a range of metaphors other than the term "God." That would get us out of the situation we often have now where everything becomes God God God God God God God God. Let's keep the justice but work at the poetry.

This is then complicated by the fact that many prayers which begin with a reference to God the Father later often have references to God the Son and God the Holy Spirit in order to make a Trinitarian witness. How will we juxtapose the male language of the Trinity with terms that proclaim the same faith but in something other than masculine terms? To complicate it even further, I would say that God is not a synonym for Father as much as it is a synonym for Trinity. God speaks more of the whole. Creator is more of a synonym for Father, but every time someone blesses in the name of Creator, Redeemer, and Sanctifier, we risk limiting our (and those who hear and take in our words to shape their notions of God) understanding of God to some smaller, functional aspect of who God is. Language is imperfect and it is always going to be imperfect, so in light of the possibility that the error of the new may be no greater than the error of the old, what will we do? We're just getting warmed up.

The third couplet is "stability" and "variety." When people become uncomfortable because somebody like me starts talking about changing how we talk about God, the antidote is to be found in this couplet. People need to have a basic stability in liturgy or they won't know how to enter it, much less infuse it with worshipful emotion. Even Pentecostals follow a stable pattern each week. But if that liturgical stability is never balanced with worshipful points of variety, the fruit can dry up and die on the vine, leaving us with only repetition. It can be as simple as changes that mark the liturgical seasons. It can be as dramatic as pulling out the pews so the space can be adapted to speak different truths. It has to be worked out locally bearing in mind that normal is what we know but growth is usually in the area of some lesser known. Wherever the point of balance is found, each community needs a measure of both in order to live. Pentecostals may find growth by doing things decently and in good order; Catholics may do the same by being attentive to the Spirit.

The fourth couplet is between two English words that have two old Greek words standing directly behind them. I'm going to introduce the Greek terms to you first because they carry the core meaning, and then the English terms, which may be easier to remember. The Greek words are *anamnesis* (a-NAM-ne-sis) and *epiclesis* (e-pi-CLEE-sis). If prayer can be understood to have an anatomy, I consider these ideas the central organs of liturgical prayer.

Christians actually borrowed *anamnesis* theology from Passover. At a Seder, the youngest child at the gathering asks, "Why is this night different from all other nights?" followed by four other questions based on the symbolism of the foods that are being eaten. The older guests answer as a way of recounting the story of how God set the Israelites free from bondage in Egypt and, in so doing, make God's saving act present now. Transferred to Christian practice, *anamnesis* is the calling forth of the past acts of God in both the Hebrew and Christian Testaments in order to make them present to us now.

> *Do this in remembrance of me*
> *We remember his death*
> *We proclaim his resurrection*
> *We await his coming in glory*

If you doubt me on this think about Holy Week, when we, too, march and sing Hosanna; we, too, get our feet washed (well, some of us anyhow); we, too, fail to wait one hour; we, too, follow from a distance like Peter; we, too, deny Jesus; we, too, shout "Crucify him!"; we, too, flee for safety; and we, too, shout, "The Lord is risen indeed. Alleluia!" Holy Week is the great *anamnesis*. As employed above, the English word most associated with *anamnesis* theology is "remembrance," so please hold onto that one. We remember in order to make present.

But we don't simply call forth the past. *Epiclesis* means "invocation" and refers to how we also call on God to do something now. In a eucharistic prayer, after a lengthy *anamnesis* of creation, the Hebrew Covenant, and the Christian Covenant, the Spirit is called down upon the gifts of bread and wine, or upon the Church universal, or upon the local assembly, or some combination of the three. In the prayer over the water in baptism, we do *anamnesis* on creation, the Red Sea, and the baptism of Jesus before the Spirit is called down to sanctify the water for the sacramental cleansing. In a collect (the prayer before the readings as well as in other places), what is asked for is often an extension into our own time of what was just remembered.

There are, however, prayer forms that are similar but require a broader meaning of the terms. While *anamnesis* normally involves an act of God in scripture, the collect for a saint's day involves something from the life of that saint. And while a liturgical *epiclesis* is normally associated with an invocation for the Holy Spirit to do something now, in other prayers the request does not always involve an action by the Spirit. For example, in a prayer of confession the remembrance is about personal or communal sin and the request is for forgiveness (which is given in the absolution). So while the concept is built on *anamnesis* and *epiclesis*, the central idea needs to be broadened to include these other forms with language that can be applied further. I suggest "remembrance" and "request." In our prayers we remember something important in order to make it present, then we ask God to do something now, often through the Holy Spirit, that makes us part of the continuing story of redemption.

Can you see it? Collects sometimes include a section on the fruit of the prayer after the request, and a word of praise after the signature. Longer forms such as eucharistic prayers have additional elements such as an opening section giving thanks or praise, an offering of the bread and wine, and a closing word of praise, but at the heart of most liturgical praying is remembrance and request. These can also guide how we pray privately and provide a way to integrate scripture into our personal prayers; reminding us that what God has done before, God can, in some measure, do in our lives now. It's a helpful way to think about everything we do in prayer, and it reminds us that being mindful of the deeper structure of prayer gives us greater security when we approach revising our prayer book.

There could be a hundred more couplets, but I hope that I have demonstrated that things we see as oppositional dichotomies can now be seen as points of tension in meaningful conversation about what is true. And the thread I would ask you to see in these four is that both sides actually need each other. The contrast makes for clearer meaning. The challenge containing the great gift is the task of finding the life-giving balance between any two for any given community. That is above the pay grade of this book, but it is important if any of this is to work and keep the Church together.

CHAPTER THREE

One Soul's Tale

A T AROUND SIX o'clock on the morning of March 29, 2007, I was woken up by my then wife who came out of the bathroom and said, "I think my water just broke." We were expecting our first child, so fair enough, but the teachers at those classes we took said that the first child is usually late so don't worry if it is (which, in my mind, meant that having two weeks until the due date meant that we really had three weeks to go and thus plenty of time, so nothing to worry about yet); I was caught unprepared both when her water broke and by how quickly our baby came. Shortly after rising, I was timing contractions. By nine o'clock, it was time to go to the birthing center.

It was a cold, clear Thursday and we got there just fine. The two midwives checked us in, took us to the room, and started to fill the tub because my wife wanted a water birth. I wasn't sure exactly what that meant, but I never found out anyway.

Did I mention that I was an extremely anxious expectant father? Mostly because I am an extremely anxious everything, but this was especially intense. And, while expectant fathers don't really have much to do other than run to various places to satisfy various cravings, I really did not have a great pregnancy. I wanted to have a child and I had a good position in a lovely parish, but as we waited for our first child to arrive, I lost my way halfway through a doctoral dissertation on the new Irish *Book of Common Prayer*. I had quit working on it because I hated it. I was actually physically unable to open the file on my computer. How could I raise a child when I couldn't even click an icon, for God's sake? My supervisor was pastoral and empathetic when I told him I was quitting; the only thing he asked of me was *not* to write the formal letter of withdrawal from the program. "Don't think about it, don't work on it, don't do anything about it, focus on your coming baby; just don't write the letter." I happily agreed because I didn't feel like doing that either. I just wanted it to *go away* so I could redirect all of my anxiety towards the baby. I remember announcing at a staff meeting the next week that I had quit the doctorate and they actually applauded. They knew it was making me miserable. I'm Irish; I do misery better than anybody I know except maybe every other member of my family.

The next thing I knew I was saying "Honey, we have a beautiful girl," and we did. That was useful information because we were old-fashioned sorts who did not want to know the gender of the child before birth. A boy was to be David because it is a family name on my side and I worked at St. David's Church. A girl was to be Elsa, because we wanted a name that was traditional but not common. Sadly, I neglected to check with the Disney corporation to find out their projected list of girl's names for upcoming movies. Trust me, in 2007, Elsa was not a common name.

She is Elsa Mary Moroney, born at 11:42 a.m., six pounds, twelve ounces, and as soon as she was born, two particularly meaningful things happened. The first was that the instant I saw her all of my anxiety immediately melted away and I said to myself, "She's a kid. I can raise a kid." Then, immediately after the midwives cut the umbilical cord, I watched as they gave her a bath and then they gave her back to her mother for feeding. Right there and then I said to myself, "The sacraments!" We are born, we are bathed, and we are fed. Birth, bath, and meal. The sacraments are not abstractions; they are rooted in original need and then ritualized in church to point to the same needs: life, cleansing, and feeding. It's all right there at birth. With that jolting epiphany, the pilot light in my doctoral oven was lit again. A week later, Elsa Mary's first trip was to the library at the Lutheran Theological Seminary at Philadelphia, where I took the old books back out again and worked faithfully at that dissertation until completion eighteen months later. Thank you, Elsa, Daddy never would have finished it without you! On August 15, 2008, on the flight back from Dublin after successfully defending my doctorate the day before, I basked in the afterglow of the previous day's victory and wrote in my journal "I HAVE BEEN RE-DEEMED!" I wrote it just like that for emphasis because I am a high school dropout, so it was a pretty big deal.

I began this chapter with that story because I have been a professional academic long enough, and have tutored enough graduate students over the years that, at least in the field of theology, there is really no such thing as objective research. We do need to strive for the highest level of objectivity possible, but God knows and deep down you and I both know that, as people of faith, we have a lot of skin in this game. It can be no other way.

Augustine of Hippo lived in the fifth century and was an important bishop and theologian of the Western Church. More recently, he has gotten himself into hot water for various and sometimes righteous reasons, which shows that the whole notion of the communion of saints means that it's never too late to get pummeled with disapproval. So while Augustine of Hippo is a complicated character, one useful thing he did do was write a book called *Confessions* in a new genre that we might call "spiritual autobiography," built on the premise that our lives are an example of how God works in the world. That's a keeper. I would only add that our theology or our beliefs are also how people of faith try to make sense out of what has happened to us throughout our lives, so the bonus prize for you reading about the liturgical theology I espouse is that I am going to 'fess up to all the things in my life I am trying to integrate and resolve by crafting this particular theology. The danger, of course, is that one little theo-slip along the way and we might get burned at the stake or, even worse, shunned on social media. I have never been able to make sense out of all the various pieces of my life. It usually feels like puzzle pieces that do not ever fit into one another. But there is one big piece that, if I put it in the middle, then all the other pieces do seem to fit around that one. Oddly enough, that big piece is worship. It's been a central part of my life for my entire life except for a six year gap during my teen years about which I take the fifth. And so should you. So, our lives are examples of how God works in the world. Perhaps when I retire. So here we go—my attempt to weave together my life in God's story.

I was born exactly nine months and seven days after John Fitzgerald Kennedy was inaugurated as the first (Irish) Catholic president of the United States. With a name like mine, you'll understand why I've always speculated that there might have been a certain celebratory quality to my conception. I have no corroboration about that but it's the closest I can come to some kind of Bible-like conception tale. That's my story and I'm sticking to it. I am the original Kennedy baby.

My parents were Depression era/World War II generation people who did not have easy upbringings. Three of my grandparents were immigrants who came here with nothing. My father lost his father and my mother lost her mother and their remaining parents were not what later generations would call "nurturing." My parents didn't give us much emotionally, but I have to remember that they gave more than they got. In lieu of hugs and caring words, they took us to church every week to get yelled at by angry celibates. I'm not kidding or exaggerating. One favorite family story is how my big brother stood up in church one Sunday right in the middle of the sermon and asked my parents (quite loudly), "What's he yelling about?" I have never wanted to teach preaching and now you know why. Too exposed. Because of that particular "methodology" in the pulpit, I have never looked for much from the sermon. I learned very young that everything I needed was in the mass itself. I liked the rhythm of it. I liked the colors of the vestments and why they changed when they changed. I just don't want the sermon to blow it. Looking back, I can see that the church was womb-like even though I kicked hard to get out of it for the first thirteen years.

Our family church was St. Teresa's in Summit, New Jersey, a big castle of a church sitting up on a hill. It has everything you would expect of a big gothic church: vaulted ceilings, stained glass windows, statues staring at you all the time and making you uncomfortable. My mother always made us sit toward the front because she liked to be close to the action. I have a few stories to tell here, so get comfortable. While ensconced one Sunday in the family pew with my brother and sister on either side, and my parents on either side of them, I had an experience that is with me still but is hard to explain. I have no idea what was going on in the mass; just the usual people talking at us. In a single second that morning, something important changed. I had the realization that I am Kevin, and being Kevin is distinct from being part of my parents or part of my brother and sister. I woke up to myself. I was self-conscious for the first time and the fact that it happened in church has never been lost on me, even if my life might've been much simpler if it had happened at the Esso station where we got the car fixed. I liked cars and maybe I should've been a mechanic. Instead, my moment happened in church so I am a priest, though not a Catholic one. I was maybe four. Simple. I was introduced to the mystery of self.

As the weeks, months, and years went by, I had to take notice of a huge stone structure that stood at the back of the altar area, with angels and archangels and all sorts of cool carvings on it. Just when we settled into our pew, a bell would ring and robed men would quietly walk out from behind this massive structure. They would talk at us for what seem like an eternity, then they would walk back around that thing and disappear as mysteriously as they had appeared. Little KJ (which is what I was called back then) would go home wondering, "Where do they come from and where do they go to?" After careful consideration, I concluded that they came from heaven, said the mass, and returned to heaven. Years later, I summoned the courage to discover that that is where the sacristy is located, but for little KJ this was the birth of the mystery of God.

God forgive me, I almost forgot Nana. The woman was God. I have never thought of God as being so much like a kind elderly man as being like a tough old Irish woman. My paternal grandmother, Margaret Casey Moroney, grew up in Kenmare, County Kerry, Ireland, and was sent to this country at the age of nineteen because she was fifth in the family, there was only one bed for the boys and one bed for the girls, and they needed room in the girls' bed for child number sixteen, who was expected soon. That was told to me by number sixteen herself, Annie Sullivan, whose only question to me about the sister she never met was, "Was she as tough as everyone says?" Yes, she was, and that tough old lady occupied the room right next to me.

Nana had found her way to Summit, New Jersey, in 1902, where she met a chauffeur by the name of Frank Moroney. They were married at the old St. Teresa's and proceeded to welcome eight children into this world, the youngest of whom was my father, Robert Casey Moroney. Frank Moroney died young. In March of 1927, he had a heart attack and was gone. My father was four. A tale was told to me by my aunt, Sr. Francis De Sales, herself a formidable woman, that when Frank died, Nana locked herself in her room for twenty-four hours, didn't see anyone or eat anything, came out the next day and set about her work, never talking about it again. Except that she died forty-five years later on the anniversary of his burial. We Irish never forget. Never.

Nana was tough. There were no "I love yous," no bouncing on the knee. She didn't hit but the woman could shake a wooden spoon at you in a way that could make you think twice. My friends were all scared of her and she liked it that way. She had old sayings like "Patience is a virtue, find it if you can, seldom in a women and never in a man." Or my favorite, "If I wanted your opinion, I'd have given it to you." She did make good hot cocoa, but you never really knew where you stood with the woman; you never knew if she loved you or what. She, too, was a mystery but in a different way because, for me, Nana was the face of God.

We all have good years and not so good years; 1972 was a horrible year. First, the best bike I ever owned was stolen from our front yard. Yes, my mother told me not to leave it in the front yard for that very reason but what ten-year-old listens to their mother about things like that? It was green with a banana seat, big handlebars and a three-speed stick shift. A Vista Torino. I rode it everywhere; after it was stolen I looked in every yard in town. Gone. And to top it all off my parents blamed me as if I was the one who stole it. No more bikes for you, KJ. You're a bad boy. Funk. I got parts from the Summit dump and built my own bike.

Next, my dad inexplicably quit his job with a wife, three young kids, and an elderly mother at home. Next thing I know the house is on the market and people are being paraded through the only home I ever knew. I loved that house; it had lots of places to play and hide. Now we were going God knows where. Actually, I don't think God knew anything at all about the place we were moving or else any sane God would have obliterated that place off the face of the earth like Sodom and Gomorrah. Horrible place. Not everyone agrees with me though. My brother still lives there forty-five years later.

Last and hardest was that Margaret Casey Moroney, eighty-eight years into this world, passed away. I remember coming downstairs one morning and, as I drew closer to the breakfast area on the porch, overhearing my parents talking about Nana dying. I burst into tears and ran back up to my room. Now I would never know what she thought of me. We went through the wake and the funeral with everybody back at the house afterwards. Eight kids (seven living), twenty-five grandkids (of which I was the twenty-fifth). That's a lot of potato faces. I know I said this already but she died on March fifteenth and years later I realized that she died on the anniversary of Frank's burial forty-five years earlier.

Two weeks later it was Easter, so we tumbled into the big green Pontiac Catalina station wagon and went to St. Teresa's. I don't remember much about the mass, but afterwards, when we were in the car driving home, I leaned forward and said to my dad, "I felt like Nana was with us in church today." Strange kid, but despite all the screaming and fighting about going to church for an entire childhood, I got it. I grasped the resurrection. Parents, do not misunderstand defiant children and do not let them kick and scream their way out of going to church. Fight the good fight. The sacraments are efficacious. Our souls are at stake. You have no idea what is getting in.

CHAPTER FOUR

Elements of a Liturgical Theology

Creatures, the Creator, and Creation

W HEN SOMEBODY USES a word like "theology" in the title they may be trying to convey a certain weight to what they are writing. "Story" and "spirituality" are fine words but they may not signal the same gravitas. "Theology" does run the risk of glazing your eyes over. I am using it deliberately because I do want to say something big. I only know how to approach the big from the small, however, and that is why I start with stories about my own spiritual upbringing. It's honest and it keeps me looking up for more. And, hopefully, it keeps you awake.

After I finished my doctorate I decided to go on a campaign to read the older theology books that were regularly referenced in the more recent books I had read. One of the most important for me was *The Idea of the Holy,* published in 1917 by a German Lutheran theologian named Rudolf Otto. It helped form my thinking about the relationship between the creation and the creator. We perceive a power greater than our own, which Otto called the numinous (from Latin, *numen*, meaning "power"); we feel vulnerable in the face of that power and we don't know what it intends for us. We feel fear (and fear means fear), awe, wonder, attraction. Otto used the Latin phrase *Mysterium tremendum et fascinans*: a tremendous mystery and fascination. God is the great mystery we intuit as power. When we experience this power we are moved both to run for safety and even more strangely to feel attracted to it. Numinous. It's a great word. Try using it in a sentence today.

Otto helped me understand why I always looked under the bed when I was a young child. It was the Boogie Man. Same feeling. When my daughter Elsa was about two and we were going through her long and highly ritualized bedtime routine, she began to end our time together by saying "Daddy, can you close the closet door on your way out?" She felt it. "Sure, sweetie." Vulnerability in the face of an intuited power whose intent is unclear. Many, if not most, if not all, of us feel that at some point. Otto's broad point is that what he called the "non-rational" aspects of religion are just as important as the "rational" aspects. Otto observed that our Enlightenment inheritance of upholding reason above all else meant that we were completely ignoring the deeper stirrings of being human. We might prefer the word "emotional" to "non-rational," but it was a hundred years ago and people were more primitive back then.

Subsequent scholars have had their go at Otto. Some argued that he was insufficiently Christian because he talked about universal human experience and emotion. Others asserted that every human being does not have this experience so he was wrong to universalize his theories. I say bunk on the first and fair enough on the second. But in the mind of this theologian, Otto gave us the place to begin our conversation about creation because, as human creatures who rightly perceive that we coexist as the weaker side of a power imbalance, we are subordinate creatures, we are creation.

Another important book for me was *The Sacred and the Profane*, written by Mircea Eliade and published in 1957. Eliade wrote in the introduction that he was picking up where Otto left off in *The Idea of the Holy*. Eliade explored, through the history of religions, how the numinous has found expression in religious culture. He also introduced a new word, *hierophany* (also from Latin), meaning "to reveal the holy," in order to describe human experiences of the divine in space and time. Building off the story of Jacob's Ladder, he showed how humans have discerned places of access with the divine. He called them axis points, seeing tall standing objects as lightning rods for divine movement. Examples abound throughout the world, some of the most obvious being totem poles, Stonehenge, and church spires, which until relatively recently would have been the highest point in any town or city. Humanity learned to see places of local presence for the divine, where this tremendous power could be honored and, on a good day, encountered in some measure through ritual reenactment. That's liturgy.

Eliade also wrote about time, which has both linear aspects (we're another year older but are we another year wiser?) and cyclical aspects (why does this keep happening to us?). He observed that, through the history of religious practice, sacred time is largely cyclical, with each day or year being a localized parallel to the beginning and end of creation, what he calls a cosmos. He cited the Native American Yokut tribe, saying that their word meaning "a year has gone by" literally means "the world has passed." Happy New Year and Happy New Creation! Eliade described liturgy as the way in which humans experience and participate in the cycles of creation. Liturgy takes the smaller in an attempt to simulate, express, and experience the bigger.

Eliade was also taken to task by subsequent scholars for over-generalizing between different peoples: Native Americans on the one hand and African tribes on the other. Fair enough, but if Otto taught us that our religious instinct is a perception of the numinous, Eliade showed that throughout history we humans have sought to participate in this creation through our cycle of rites. Once again, we are creatures, but we are creatures with bigger brains that give us the ability to reflect and create in ways that other creature siblings cannot. And one of the primary ways that we have done this throughout time is by means of what Christians call liturgy or worship.

One goal of this book, and the particular goal of this

chapter, is to change the starting point for liturgical theology. There are in fact many ways to study liturgy. Anglican discourse tends to be heavy on history and this is as true with liturgy as with other areas. The 1549 prayer book said this. The 1552 prayer book said that. I'm trying not to do that. Other ways to study liturgy include a sociological approach; studying what Christians do when they are together. Mentioned earlier was a mentor of mine, Gordon Lathrop, who writes about liturgy as an extension of biblical theology. I have taught from that perspective for years, and I want to keep that but back the process up one step to begin liturgical theology at creation. I know that any discussion of creation normally focuses on the question of "Where did all this come from?" turning to Genesis or science, but I want to follow Otto and Eliade by beginning a creation theology with human perception and in that way begin liturgical theology with creation. In the far reaches of human history, all theology had to begin with some reflection on our being and early human liturgical practice had to begin as a reflection on our existence. One of life's indisputable facts is that we exist, unless we want to start questioning our sensory perception. Our bodies exist. Our sense of self-awareness exists. The people, animals, plants, and trees around us exist. The earth, the atmosphere, the sun, moon, and stars exist. And God only knows what else exists.

I have no argument with science. In one sense, both theology and science are forms of observation from different periods of human history or from different cultures. Ironically, it is my daughter Maggie who often helps me work through my own beliefs by making me explain things. She is named Margaret after Nana, and is the seventh Margaret in our family. My grandmother, my aunt, three cousins, my sister, and now my daughter. It was important for me to name my daughter after the woman who, in so many ways, represented God to me. One day, not too long ago, I was driving Maggie to a play date and she initiated a conversation I had been waiting for since my girls started school. Like most priest's kids they had gone to church since birth so they had heard the church's story many times. Now they are learning new stories and need to work out the relationship between them. Maggie, now age eleven, said, "Dad, I'm having trouble in science; I just don't understand evolution."

Gimme da ball. I talked about how religion and science are two different ways of thinking about our origins, but that they don't need to be viewed as being in conflict; they can both contribute to our understanding. I reminded Maggie that we say that the sun rises each morning because that is how it looks, but science has taught us that the earth actually rotates on its axis to a point where the part of the planet we live on is exposed to the light of the sun. We know that's true but we still describe how it looks because it's simpler.

She countered, "I don't understand the Big Bang."

Deep breath. "Well, sweetie, life comes from energy, and light is energy. When you have a lot of energy you have to run around and play to use it. The Big Bang is a little like that; it was an explosion of energy so big that it formed the universe and is still going out and out even today. The Bible says something similar. The first thing

God said in the Bible was 'Let there be light,' which is like the Big Bang when you think about it; light is energy."

"I still don't understand," she said.

Sigh. "Me, neither" said I.

The next morning Maggie was heading out the door for school and she said "Pray for me in science today, Dad."

"You got it, sweetie." I'll take it.

Anatomically modern humans buried their dead in caves 120 thousand years ago, and in what is now Iraq a Neanderthal was buried in a garland of flowers sixty thousand years ago. They must have been reflecting on something to do with life and death. Perhaps even where we come from and where we go to. Just like me at St. Teresa's.

I prefer viewing creation from the vantage point of perception because it takes us from abstractions about origins down into the nitty gritty of our own lives. I have spent my share of time on therapist's couches, and one exercise I was led through early on was to reflect back to my earliest memory in life. The dimmest, darkest shadow of a memory was of the wind in my face with my dad behind me, just over my right shoulder. I didn't know exactly what the memory was until I told it to my big sister who said, "That must be the toy roller coaster we had in the back yard in Summit. Dad used to push us on it all the time." As she described it, the picture came more into focus with little rises and falls as my father pushed me along. Two things are remarkable about that memory. If my sister is right, then that memory is from before I turned two, because we moved from that house one month before my second birthday. The other thing is that it explains how, for as long as I have been alive, I have loved the feeling of the wind in my face. Going back to my earliest memory and reaching all the way forward to this very moment.

When I began to emerge from a years-long depression, my doctor told me that I had to exercise more to get the tension out of my body. It was difficult to find time to exercise because I work full time and parent full time, which means that I am pretty well occupied from 7:00 a.m. until 9:00 p.m. each day. A couple of weeks later, I got an idea that came to me from my early self, although I didn't realize it at the time. I started getting up before dawn and taking my bike out for an early morning ride in the direction of the sunrise which, in Manhattan, means various points on the East River. I loved it immediately. It reminded me of how much I loved riding my bike as a child and within a few days of beginning that new exercise program, I was drawn back into my life's earliest memory. Having the wind in my face makes me feel awake and alive and aware of my existence. It helps me see that it is good to be alive. I perceive the numinous. I experience the holy. This is my personal creation story and it changes how I view everything around me. I will ride till I die and I will care for everywhere I ride.

My larger theological point in all these layers of awareness is that they are expanding versions of the same gift: home. Body = home. House or apartment = home. Town, region, and state (or whatever equivalent you have) = home. Earth = home. Universe = home. That is an orientation towards creation theology but also a call to address our creation emergency. I believe that biblically-centered people took a deadly turn when we read Genesis and declared ourselves "The rulers of creation!" Episcopalians say just that in Eucharistic Prayers C and D (yes, I know that D also says that we should serve). First of all, Genesis doesn't say that we rule all of creation anyway. It does say that God gave us "dominion" over the other creatures of the earth, but try that one next time you meet a shark in the water or a bear in the woods. And I don't think victims of earthquakes or tsunamis feel anything like rulers. That's the kind of thing that is written by people who feel powerful. More importantly, one of these days when I have more time I am going to do a word study on the Hebrew term *mashal*, often translated "dominion"—I suspect that I will find that there is *care* included in the meaning of that term and not just *free license* to do whatever we want. We baby boomers with our plastics (remember that scene in *The Graduate?*) and our never-ending pursuit of adventure and comfort via planes, automobiles, and air conditioning may have done more to destroy this planet than every other generation in the history of the world combined. Honestly, my own epiphany about all this was not until a few years ago when news agencies started to show pictures of the continent-sized blobs of plastic garbage floating around in the ocean. Yes we did, yes we still are, and we better start thinking of ways to do something about it before we have no home at all. We can start by coming up with a better word than "ruler" to describe our relationship to the rest of creation.

Me also think'st it is getting late in the game for us Episcopalians to begin our catechism with "Human Nature" as the planet's average temperature rises, the ice caps melt, the seas rise in both volume and temperature, the ferocity of storms increases, and FEMA is running out of money. We are creatures who have knowingly or unknowingly done catastrophic damage to the home we share with countless other creatures who cannot match our capacity for creativity or destruction. Our catechism and our liturgical theology need to start with creation because we have to teach in order to change. The way in which industrialized humans have viewed themselves in relation to the rest of creation is wrong wrong wrong wrong wrong wrong. Though I try to keep an open mind about it.

The big problem, as I see it, was illustrated in a speech given at my church after the collapse of the economy in 2008. The speaker was Jack Bogle, an independent thinker and the founder of the Vanguard Group, a top-shelf investment company. During the Q & A, someone asked how the economic collapse could have happened when mortgage companies had to know that so many people did not have the capacity to pay pack their loans and thus would have to default. Jack paused in thought for a moment and said one of the truest truths I have ever heard: "It is hard to speak the truth when the lie is making you so much money." Somebody is making a lot of money off the destruction of our planet so it is going to be very hard to speak the truth. Those who have ears to hear . . .

We start liturgical theology with creation because creation is where God started with us and worship began as a response to that. We start liturgical theology with creation because our first reflection on how to address God is that God is our Creator. We start liturgical theology with creation because we are at our most basic level a part of creation; we are members of creation. Please somebody find a better word than ruler! We start liturgical theology with creation because if we as humans do not begin serious repentance (which means turning which means changing our behavior), then we will be in serious trouble on this planet and we will be responsible for that before God our Creator. Amen. And yet our liturgies say very little about creation, our churches have very little intentional creation-oriented symbolism. It's almost as if we are jumping to the end of the story with our crosses and pulpits and fonts and altars (all great) without doing the harder work of where we began (not so great). It is indeed hard to speak the truth when the lie is keeping us cozily tucked into our dominant culture. But it is getting late, my fellow creature-friends, so we better learn to start at the beginning.

Postscript

This chapter was completed to this point on Monday, February 24, 2020. Two weeks later, COVID-19 began to force communities all over the world to go into lockdown. Many churches were closed on March 12 and had three days to figure out what to do come Sunday. The original projection was that we would be closed for three weeks but we were really only beginning to see what was to come (bear in mind I am writing from New York City). In an article published in *The Guardian* on March 25, just as we were settling into stay-at-home orders, Inger Andersen, the environmental chief for the United Nations, was quoted as saying that "humanity was placing too many pressures on the natural world with damaging consequences," and that "our continued erosion of wild spaces has brought us uncomfortably close to animals and plants that harbor diseases that can jump to humans." She noted that 75 percent of all emerging infectious diseases come from wildlife. In other words, it is neither a Chinese virus nor a European virus, it is a virus born of careless human incursion into the natural habitat; our consumption of space and wild animal life for our own purposes. COVID-19 is a direct result of our heresy of intention to rule the earth and all its creatures. We don't hear much talk about that, do we now?

There have been many horrors to this crisis, but it has also provided us with unique opportunities. Faith communities that were catapulted into online services learned quickly that they might actually reach more people that way. Many people who were forced to stay at home realized that they had needed to slow down for a long time. And what is the opportunity for the Church? The Greek word *metanoia*, a word traditionally translated as "repentance" or "conversion," was used in the gospels of Matthew, Mark, and Luke and in the book of Acts to describe a change of mind, a change of behavior, a turning. Let's not go all the way back. Let's begin planning ways we can slow down the things that are harmful to the planet. In the weeks following the lockdown, global observers reported cleaner air and cleaner water. Without planes, trains, and automobiles billowing their pollution into our skies the earth was better for it. The problem, of course, was that it was not good for the economy, but an economy can be restructured. A planet cannot. The opportunity for the Church is a call to change our minds and behaviors and turn toward understanding ourselves as fellow inhabitants on this planet, not rulers. COVID-19 underscores the importance of beginning with good creation theology.

CHAPTER FIVE

Elements of a Liturgical Theology
The Bible

MOVING FROM CREATION to scripture in liturgical theology is about moving from the universal to the more particular. We're not home yet but we are now entering our continent. In another context we would move to Torah or Quran or whatever anybody else counts as sacred writ. But for us it is the Bible that contains our primordial stories, the creation and early narratives of Jewish and Christian people. If you learn enough to get under the skin of the Bible you will find that it also gives us the stories that teach us how to wrestle with every meaningful question in life, but that takes more work and, in my experience, not enough Episcopalians appear interested in going that deep. My point is that you should; it'll save your life.

The Christian liturgy is where the Church tells her story, and this story should show care and intention in taking us through themes of creation and then moving us into the symbolic universe of biblical stories, both Hebrew and Christian, which we often call the old and the new. This, of course, is not new. We have done it for so long and in so many ways that the real question is whether the permeation of the scriptures in our liturgies has become white noise; something we have heard and seen for so long that we no longer hear or see it. We have incorporated scripture in at least four ways: the space, the language of prayer, the readings and proclamation, and the sacraments. It may be helpful to dust these off and see if they offer new teaching opportunities for the benefit of God's children.

There are different kinds of Christian liturgical spaces with different theologies at play in each. Most of us recognize classically sacramental buildings very well: All those beautiful dark stained-glass-windowed churches with altars in the center to proclaim the sacramental orientation to those who enter. The classic evangelical space generally places the pulpit in the center to declare its emphasis on the proclamation on the word. These spaces are often more plain but can be adorned just as lavishly as the sacramental churches. Modern communal churches put us in a circle to emphasize the gathered community and tend to keep symbols limited to the essentials of word and sacrament. What they all share in common is that each attempts to teach scripture in slightly varying ways.

I was once rector of a beautiful gothic church, Christ Church, Ithan, Pennsylvania, and the scheme of the stained glass windows displayed the entire life of Christ around the space: annunciation, birth, baptism, calling of the disciples, transfiguration, last supper, crucifixion, resurrection, great commission, ascension, ending with a window of Jesus on the stormy sea with his disciples, meaning *us*. You bet I used those windows to teach kids, and the grown-ups paid attention too. It is also not accidental that people sit in the "nave" of a church (from the Latin *navis*, meaning boat), with the roof looking a lot like an upside-down hull of a ship, not unlike the one that Noah and his family were saved on. The primary symbols of such a building highlight a lectern and/or pulpit (word), a font (baptism) and an altar (Eucharist) as symbols of scripture. Put them all together and you have direct citations in the windows, allusions to scripture in the architectural design, and symbolic representations of scripture in the hardware of the space. The other architectural forms work with the same material but adjust the dials a bit. The evangelical church turns up the auditory elements of the word. The modern communal turns up the sense of a gathered community around the central symbols. All are great and all can be tools for teaching scriptural narrative to people but how often do we actually do that?

Jeanne Halgren Kilde showed us in her book *Sacred Power, Sacred Space* that the things we emphasize in our worship spaces are power statements. That does not make them wrong *per se*, but when she writes about how the construction and layout of our spaces reflect our ideas about divine power (vaulted ceilings), clerical power (elevated pulpits, seats, and altars), and people power (lower seats), then we should probably give consideration to whether the architecture, symbols, and furniture of our sacred spaces are making the statements about power that we say we believe and intend. Failure to do so could result in the unthinkable outcome of suggesting that clergy are closer to God than laity. We would never do that, would we?

The language of prayer is often rich with scriptural citation or allusions. Anglicans know this well whether they know it or not. "The peace of God which passes all understanding . . . " is Philippians 4. "We are not worthy so much as to gather the crumbs under thy table . . . " is Jesus with the Syrophoenician woman (Mark 7:24–30). Remembrance is often the scriptural fulcrum on which many of our most beloved prayers rest.

In the mid- to late first century, a teacher produced a document we know as the *Didache*, the first part of which is a catechism built around material that reads a lot like the Sermon on the Mount (Matthew 5:1–7:29). In the mid-second century someone named Justin who was later martyred (thus known as Justin Martyr) wrote about gatherings that included the "writings of the prophets" and the "memoirs of the apostles." By the sixteenth century, Thomas Cranmer, founder and architect of the Anglican prayer book tradition, wrote that the entire Bible should be read through in church during a year and he just about made that happen. In his first lectionary for daily prayer (which he intended everyone to use), the Hebrew Bible was read through once, the New Testament three times, and the Psalms every month. There was also the eucharistic lectionary, which included only an Epistle and Gospel reading (no reading from the Hebrew scriptures back then).

What most of us use today is the Revised Common Lectionary (RCL), a three-year cycle of readings that gets more scriptures read in our public assemblies than has ever been true before. The only problem is that while it is absolutely brilliant for those who know scripture, it is of very little help to those who do not, which, we now know, is most of us. When the lector in church announces a reading from the book of the prophet Isaiah, what does that mean to you? For some, it transports us back into the Babylonian exile of the Jewish people, a time of deep existential crisis that miraculously inspired them to look ahead to God's restoration. That's if you know your Bible. For the rest of us, you might as well talk about your aunt Lydia because we have no notion of who Isaiah was or that prophecy was actually poetic preaching more than fortune telling. And a preacher cannot be expected to illuminate all three readings in every sermon. It is imperative for us to teach and learn the scriptures so that we are able to receive the benefits of our cycle of readings.

I have already shown my cards on proclamation (remember the stories about the Catholic priests of my childhood?) and I'm not saying I'm right, only that my personal history turned me out my own way. With that said, I do a lot of preaching, and it goes like this. The readings are the *anamnetic,* or remembrance, portion of the work and the proclamation / sermon / homily is the *epiclectic* part, where we call down the Spirit and get a theme or two or three of something that is going on in the readings that can be activated in the minds and lives of those who are listening. The sermon is an important part of our liturgical anatomy; every study of people looking for churches clearly shows how important it is, and when it is working well it both points back to the scriptures just heard and forward to the prayers and the table and to life back out in the world.

And now for something completely sacramental. On the one hand we have had the stability of bath and meal, baptism and Eucharist, for two thousand years and that is remarkable. On the other hand we have believed so many different things about those two sacraments that it's almost a miracle to accept that we're talking about the same two things. But we are. Christianity was not the only bath and meal fellowship in first-century Judaism, you know. The community rule at Qumran, the place where the Dead Sea Scrolls were found, says that no one gets to participate in the sacred meal each day without undergoing the ritual cleansing. Ritual as opposed to real. They were out in the desert and the only time water came was when they had their periodic large rain storms, so that water could sit in those basins for a long time without getting, shall we say, refreshed. Christianity developed a bit differently. In order to join John the Baptist's movement you had to be baptized. While that was going on, Jesus was walking all over the place teaching and healing and feeding or being fed. Both were drawing pretty good crowds. We are also told that Jesus was a bit of a foodie.

He got invited to a lot of meals and wasn't too picky about who else was there: the gospels make a big deal about how accepting he was of people who did not live the best lives. John gets killed, a bunch of his followers go over to the Jesus movement, and next thing you know that first-century document, the *Didache*, says that you are not getting to the sacred meal unless you have been baptized. Any study of movements that join together will show you that the group that is joining the other one will always bring something with them. So now the early Jesus people start getting picky about who they eat with as baptism becomes a part of their regular practice.

When you walk into most churches that fit into the categories described above (sacramental, evangelical, communal), there is usually an altar or a holy table either in the most prominent position or, in the classic evangelical style, slightly subordinate to the pulpit. Early Christians continued the meal fellowship of Jesus, and over the first thousand years of Christian history the Eucharist evolved from being a full meal to a sacrament to a sacrifice, with theological development that led us from "eucharisticized" bread and wine in Justin Martyr in the second century (bread and wine that had been given thanks over) to transubstantiation by the thirteenth century (the flour and water don't change but what they are does change). The sixteenth-century reformers attempted to recapture the sense of a meal, and the Liturgical Movement of the twentieth century made further attempts to do the same, but we are left with what often happens in liturgy: we are confronted with layers of tradition. So today where the altar stands, what it is made of, how it is adorned, and how seating is arranged can reflect the different layers of the history of the space and of the particular denominational or theological perspective in which it participates. Complicated, I know. Regardless, in most spaces, when you enter a Christian church, the altar or table will either be the first or second central symbol of the space. The meal that became a sacrament that became a sacrifice that, in Anglicanism, became the *anamnesis* of Christ's sacrifice and our sacrifice of praise and thanksgiving in which we offer ourselves, our souls and bodies in response to what Christ did for us, this Eucharist became the theological gathering place for all the great themes of scripture. Read any composed eucharistic prayer, especially in the Book of Common Prayer's Rite II (BCP 361–375). The great themes are all there: Creation, sin, Israel, incarnation, the ministry of Jesus, the cross, the resurrection.

You may recall that I noted earlier that I have always found the gospel more than adequately proclaimed in the liturgy, and that comes together most clearly when the great biblical themes are presented in word and symbol and action in baptism and eucharist. Here is my final point about the scriptural foundation of the liturgy: I believe that scripture does and should permeate every aspect of Christian worship. But if that is the case, then why are most Episcopalians biblically illiterate? Can it be that something that is everywhere can soon feel like it is nowhere and thus become lost? Whatever the case, how can we teach the Bible and its importance to those who have no background with it? First, it seems to me, is that we teach scripture to people who are interested in learning the Bible (and that might mean teaching a hunger for scripture needs to precede teaching the Bible itself).

The other answer is that we as leaders need to teach in a way that is not some elemental version of Trivial Pursuit, but does in fact get under people's skin and demonstrates that the themes told through these stories are important to people's lives. Teach the windows, teach the architecture, teach the symbols, teach the stories, talk about how complicated our lives are but how baptism reminds us that in Christ we are made clean despite all that soils us and that in Christ we are fed to go back out into the madness and try again. And then we come back and pray and give thanks and talk about how we did this time.

I currently serve as priest-in-residence at St. Peter's in Clifton, New Jersey. I first showed up there in November 2017 thinking I'd be there for a few weeks. I sit here twenty-seven months later loving and being loved by those people. Trust me, there is no process that can really tell us when a community and a priest are going to click this well. We all know it's impermanent, but it is good. Really good. I know that I am loved. Lent was coming up and I proposed a "Prayer Challenge" where, during the week, we prayed a simplified version of Morning Prayer from the BCP with readings from Luke's gospel that were broken up into a seven-week, five-day lectionary devised by *moi* and then on Sundays we talked about what we read. So we prayed together but in our own spaces, and we read on our own but brought it together on Sunday. Pretty much everybody signed up. Then, when our churches were shut down due to COVID-19 and everything went online, we already had something in place that kept us connected, praying and worshipping together. So a program that was intended for Lent remained in place for another six months and we read our way through Luke, Genesis, and women of the Bible. Would it work everywhere? No; nothing does. But it worked here, and for that I am very grateful. You might want to try it, or something like it.

So the task before us is to get the Bible under people's skin so they can see that it is about their lives as presented through the symbolic universe of a library of ancient sacred books that show how God called to humanity through a small, historically obscure people known as Israel and then, in an even more focused way, though an historically obscure person known as Jesus of Nazareth. We might understand it as Israel = Us and the Word made flesh = God became one of Us. God is always trying to reach Us. Scripture as song, as readings, as proclamation, as prayer, and as sacrament connects people back to God so they can go out with new tools to live the Christian life in this world.

CHAPTER SIX

Elements of a Liturgical Theology

The Ordos of Christian Liturgy

WE'VE CONSIDERED CREATION as a starting point and discussed scripture—and its symbols—as forming a frame for liturgy, and now we're going to talk about liturgy itself, though perhaps not in a way that seems familiar. Rather than pick at where you put the announcements or whether you sing the Doxology, we are going to look at the anatomy of Christian worship. Much of what we experience in liturgical worship grew out of scripture and took shape in the first centuries of the Christian Church. With some modifications over time, that form, that shape, that *ordo* is with us still every time we gather. It's like taking an x-ray of our services to see what is going on underneath the skin. We will rely heavily on the work of Gordon Lathrop in regards to ordo, but also on Thomas O'Loughlin's book, *The Didache,* to further understand its origins with my theological reflection to expand upon these premises.

In his book *Holy Things*, Lathrop notes that from the point of origin Christian liturgy has followed a deep pattern that "evokes and replicates the deep structure of biblical language, the use of the old to say the new by means of juxtaposition." New meaning coming out of the tension between the two. He calls this deep pattern *ordo*. But there are many old/new juxtapositions that create numerous ordos. He notes the weekday/eighth day juxtaposition, meaning daily prayer and Sunday meal. He cites what he calls the "basic Christian liturgical dualism" in the word/meal juxtaposition, where the liturgy of the word from the ancient Jewish synagogue was married to the meal of the young Jesus movement and where, as Lathrop described it, the old was broken and given gospel meaning in the new. Jewish people kept the old practice but added to it the new.

Early Christianity was not only coupled with ancient Judaism, the first-century Church was also an amalgamation of two simultaneous Jewish movements in first-century Palestine: the Baptist Movement and the Jesus movement. John the Baptist worked from the south and focused on proclamation that led to a baptism of repentance for the forgiveness of sin as a way to prepare for the coming Kingdom of God. Jesus came from the north and focused on teaching, healing, feeding, and preparing for the Kingdom of God by following him.

There are parallels between John's orientation towards the coming Messiah and how to prepare for it and another movement out in the desert at Qumran where a group known as the Essenes removed themselves from society, lived in the wilderness, and prepared for the coming Messiah by living a rigorous life in a bath and meal society. Every day members of Qumran needed to undergo a ritual bath in order to attend the sacred meal. Like John, their documents talk about preparing the way for the Messiah in the wilderness, quoting Isaiah 40, but there was one big difference between John and the Essenes. Out in the wilderness of Qumran, once you joined that community you stayed, waiting for divine intervention; they viewed society as being so evil that they separated themselves completely. John, however, went back as if to rescue people from a burning building. He proclaimed and baptized his way as far as King Herod's house, where he met his end.

Jesus was more of a foodie. He traveled from town to town teaching and healing and getting invited to meals where he generally offended people by cavorting with the dark sheep of Israel or, even worse, doing something kind on the Sabbath when you weren't supposed to do any activity (this was before market economy got everybody running all the time).

The gospels do their best to work out a seamless relationship between the two. Mark, the earliest gospel, cast John as the foreordained forerunner to Jesus, as do

Matthew and John. Luke casts them as cousins. I know some people get antsy when somebody like me starts questioning the historicity of anything that is ever written in scripture, but you know as well as I do that things are never that clear when they are actually happening and I don't think the weaving together of these two movements and their leaders is any different. There were two simultaneous messianic movements that had some thematic overlap in first-century Palestine. The leader of the first got killed by Herod and then at least some of his followers transferred membership to the Jesus movement. If you study movements and how they work, you will find that when one movement is amalgamated into another they always bring something with them that becomes part of the new fused movement. The Baptists brought their water bath, which may be why all four gospel writers placed the baptism of Jesus at the beginning of each gospel, even though baptism does not seem to have otherwise been a major concern of Jesus or his movement. It is cast as a kind of passing of the torch that then justifies people moving from the one movement to the other, as scripture testifies to in John 1:37. Then silence.

This, then, changes the way we see the presentation of liturgical material and their pattern of ordo in one of our earliest Christian documents. *The Didache* begins with a six-chapter catechism that began its life as a Jewish document called *The Two Ways* but was altered to accommodate Christian use. The catechism leads to two chapters on fasting and baptism, three chapters on Eucharist, and five chapters on matters relating to community life.

The baptismal material is fascinating because it

combines material that is both adamant in its terms in verse one, followed by material that is highly flexible in verses two to four:

> **7:1** Concerning baptism, you should baptize this way: After hearing all these things, baptize in the name of the Father, and of the Son, and of the Holy Spirit, in flowing water.
>
> **7:2** But if you have no running water, baptize in other water; and if you cannot do so in cold water, then in warm.
>
> **7:3** If you have very little, pour water three times on the head in the name of Father and Son and Holy Spirit.
>
> **7:4** Before the baptism, both the baptizer and the candidate for baptism, plus any others who can, should fast. The candidate should fast for one or two days beforehand.[4]

This coupling of the adamant and the flexible suggest layers of composition; most likely an earlier layer from a more rigorous group of Jewish Christians, perhaps those who also edited the *Two Ways* document, tempered later by more flexible Jewish Christians who were adapting to different circumstances and perhaps a new audience of Gentiles. Both old and new remain as is the consistent

---

4   Thomas O'Loughlin, *The Didache: A Window on the Earliest Christians* (Grand Rapids: Baker, 2010).

Christian pattern: the new breaking and giving meaning to the old.

> **9:1** Concerning the Eucharist, give thanks this way.

> **9:2** First, concerning the cup: We thank you, our Father, for the holy vine of David your servant, which you made known to us through Jesus your servant. To you be the glory forever.

> **9:3** Next, concerning the broken bread: We thank you, our Father, for the life and knowledge which you made known to us through Jesus your servant. To you be the glory forever.

> **9:4** Even as this broken bread was scattered over the hills, and was gathered together and became one, so let your church be gathered together from the ends of the earth into your kingdom. To you is the glory and the power through Jesus Christ forever.

> **9:5** Allow no one to eat or drink of your Eucharist, unless they have been baptized in the name of the Lord. For concerning this, the Lord has said, "Do not give what is holy to dogs."

> **10:1** After the Eucharist when you are filled, give thanks this way:

10:2 We thank you, holy Father, for your holy name which you enshrined in our hearts, and for the knowledge and faith and immortality that you made known to us through Jesus your servant. To you be the glory forever.

10:3 You, Master Almighty, have created all things for your name's sake. You gave food and drink to all people for enjoyment, that they might give thanks to you; but to us you freely give spiritual food and drink and life eternal through Jesus, your servant.

10:4 Before all things we thank you because you are mighty. To you be the glory forever.

10:5 Remember, Lord, your church. Deliver it from all evil and make it perfect in your love, and gather it from the four winds sanctified for your kingdom which you have prepared for it. For Yours is the power and the glory forever.

10:6 Let grace come, and let this world pass away! Hosanna to the Son of David! If anyone is holy, let him come; if anyone is not holy, let him repent. Maranatha! Amen.

10:7 But permit the prophets to make thanksgiving as much as they desire.

The eucharistic material has long perplexed liturgical scholars because it does not reflect the long-held theories regarding the origins of the Eucharist in the Last Supper. More recently, it has forced us to reconsider those theories to see a more diverse line of development. Yet here, for the first time, we see a clearly stated requirement for baptism prior to Eucharist that took hold and has remained the primary pattern ever since: "Allow no one to eat or drink of your Eucharist, unless they have been baptized." This could easily send us off into a discussion about what we now call "open communion," but that is not my purpose here. You do what seems right to you. O'Loughlin reflected on the question of who might create such a requirement, and his proposed answer was the Baptists coming over after the demise of their movement. The community of the *Didache* may have included a strong remnant of former Baptists, and this could then explain both the rubric requiring the ritual bath prior to the sacred meal, as well as the placement of the scriptural and baptismal ordo in the primary position prior to the meal, which would in turn explain the phenomenon of a slightly different ordo to include a triplet of word/bath/ meal that can then be traced through documents titled "Church Orders" throughout antiquity. The amalgamation of the two movements might explain the very early development of what I will call the initiation ordo, which appears to be parallel in time very early with Lathrop's primary word/meal ordo.

In the mid-second century, a Christian teacher named Justin explained his faith and practice by describing the same pattern in an even more developed way:

> 61. As many as are persuaded and believe that what we teach and say is true, and undertake to be able to live accordingly, are instructed to pray and to entreat God with fasting, for the remission of their sins that are past, we praying and fasting with them. Then they are brought by us where there is water, and are regenerated in the same manner in which we were ourselves regenerated. For, in the name of God, the Father and Lord of the universe, and of our Saviour Jesus Christ, and of the Holy Spirit, they then receive the washing with water.

> 65. But we, after we have thus washed him who has been convinced and has assented to our teaching, bring him to the place where those who are called brethren are assembled, in order that we may offer hearty prayers in common for ourselves and for the baptized [illuminated] person . . . Having ended the prayers, we salute one another with a kiss. There is then brought to the president of the brethren bread and a cup of wine mixed with water; and he taking

them, gives praise and glory to the Father of the universe, through the name of the Son and of the Holy Ghost, and offers thanks at considerable length for our being counted worthy to receive these things at His hands. And when he has concluded the prayers and thanksgivings, all the people present express their assent by saying Amen.

66. And this food is called among us Eukaristia [the Eucharist], of which no one is allowed to partake but the [one] who believes that the things which we teach are true, and who has been washed with the washing that is for the remission of sins, and unto regeneration, and who is so living as Christ has enjoined. For not as common bread and common drink do we receive these; but in like manner as Jesus Christ our Saviour, having been made flesh by the Word of God, had both flesh and blood for our salvation, so likewise have we been taught that the food which is blessed by the prayer of his word, and from which our blood and flesh by transmutation are nourished, is the flesh and blood of that Jesus who was made flesh.

This, of course, does not take away from the equal primacy of eucharistic theology and practice. The *Didache* and Justin also describe the ordo for Sunday gatherings:

Didache:

> **14:1** On the Lord's day, gather yourselves together and break bread, give thanks, but first confess your sins so that your sacrifice may be pure. **14:2** However, let no one who is at odds with his brother come together with you, until he has reconciled, so that your sacrifice may not be profaned.

Justin:

> And on the day called Sunday, all who live in cities or in the country gather together to one place, and the memoirs of the apostles or the writings of the prophets are read, as long as time permits; then, when the reader has ceased, the president verbally instructs, and exhorts to the imitation of these good things. Then we all rise together and pray, and, as we before said, when our prayer is ended, bread and wine and water are brought, and the president in like manner offers prayers and thanksgivings, according to his ability, and the people assent, saying Amen; and there is a distribution to each, and a participation of that over which thanks have

been given, and to those who are absent a portion is sent by the deacons. And they who are well to do, and willing, give what each thinks fit; and what is collected is deposited with the president, who succours the orphans and widows and those who, through sickness or any other cause, are in want, and those who are in bonds and the strangers sojourning among us, and in a word takes care of all who are in need.

All these texts from the *Didache* and Justin provide two distinct sets of liturgies we still have with us today. The first are initiatory baptismal Eucharists and the second are Sunday Eucharists. I consider both of these primary ordo; the patterns of Christian worship that go back to our point of origin. Word, bath, and meal; word and sacrament. The "word" does appear in varied forms, but I do not consider that as important as the universal inclusion of some form of the word. The bath falls between word and meal because these early Christians, perhaps drawing on their Qumran/Baptist lineage, saw the ritual bath as the door to the sacred meal.

The reason it is worth viewing the development of the ordo in this way is because it sets baptismal theology and practice at the same level of importance as the Eucharist. In the following centuries, and continuing until relatively recently, baptismal practice became more of a private matter, following the theology of original sin. "Make sure the kid is baptized quickly just in case, God forbid, anything should happen to the baby." This development moved baptism out of its primary position and into a private place, where it remained until liturgical theologians of the twentieth century made it a matter of primary importance to reinstate baptismal theology and practice to its central place as constituting Christian identity and ministry; a renewed emphasis that we continue to teach and implement to this day.

A further benefit of seeing both sets as the earliest developmental pattern of ordo is that it means we are not limited to one of what we would later call sacramental actions. The word-bath-meal ordo gives us a biblical pattern of how to work with new needs such as healing rites, commissioning rites, ash rites, house blessings, confessions, all other sacramental rites that can stand either on their own or can lead to Eucharist.

If there is truth in this, then it also suggests an even more primordial layer of ordo, even before we get to the particulars of juxtaposing old and new or word and meal. Lathrop places a value on speaking of these important things in their natural terms. Bath and meal rather than baptism and Eucharist. Old and new. Stripping them down to their original forms removes later layers of accumulated belief, but we can then miss the intention behind why Christians past and Christians now place the old alongside the new. It is not only because we continue what we have known and add to it; it is not only breaking the old and giving it new meaning. We are also remembering what God has done in the past, which then leads to us praying that God will do something similar now. The language of old and new needs to be poured into the wineskin of remembrance and request, *anamesis* and *epiclesis*: words introduced earlier in this book and arguably the most basic couplet of any ordo of Christian liturgy.

As I noted earlier, Lathrop also pointed out that there is a week/Sunday juxtaposition; the week referring to daily prayer. Paul Bradshaw has written that the basic pattern for weekday prayer was of psalms/hymns and prayers. In the basilicas of Roman cities, this was envisioned as a parallel to the morning and evening sacrifices of the now destroyed temple in Jerusalem and included only a limited number of psalms that were repeated. By contrast, in the austerity of the Egyptian desert they strove to fulfill the mandate from St. Paul to pray unceasingly through the ongoing recitation of psalms in order followed by meditative prayer. Eventually the two traditions merged, with the fixed psalms/hymns used for the opening, followed by the cyclical reading of psalms, followed by prayer. This third ordo remains important to Anglican liturgy in the Daily Offices of the Book of Common Prayer.

While we could easily produce a thousand-page book to review the changes that have been made to liturgical texts over two thousand years, it is still meaningful to know, in much shorter terms, that our prayer texts down through the centuries have been held in the arms of a patterned way of praying that traces back to our scriptural roots. We now call this patterned way of praying "ordo" as a reminder that we have been gifted with this word, this bath, this meal, which we surround with gathering and sending rites at beginning and end, in order to root us in what God has done in Christ so that fruit can be born in us now.

CHAPTER SEVEN

Elements of an Anglican Liturgical Theology

The Book of
Common Prayer

The good ol' BCP
Yes that's the book for me
I stand alone on the word of Tom
The good ol' BCP
(Sung to the tune of "The B-I-B-L-E")

D O YOU KNOW that the history of the media form
known as a book is intimately connected to the
history of Christianity? In the first century CE, Jewish
and Christian people both used the scroll form that had

come from Egypt. For example, in the second Epistle to Timothy the author asked for scrolls and parchments to be brought. Unfortunately, scrolls could be difficult to travel with and early Christianity was a missionary movement with itinerants traveling around the Mediterranean world. While we have no record of exactly when or where it happened, by the early second century Christian missionaries must have seen Roman merchants who used an accounting booklet called a codex, something like a small notepad to us, and said "Hey Seamus, let's use that!" In a very short period of time it became the preferred media form and with that the book was conceived.

As the Christian faith spread over the next several centuries, intentional Christian communities called monasteries were formed and, as settled faith communities, their buildings included rooms called *scriptora*, spaces dedicated to copying the scriptures and other sacred books. As century gave way to century, binding was developed to allow for more pages to be gathered together and the process of illumination—artistic renderings of text and fanciful characters—developed to bring artistic beauty to the book.

At the same time, liturgies and books to govern them were also developing. In the first century, the *Didache* reflected very simple liturgies, with brief rubrics saying, "When you give thanks, do it this way. . . ." By the high Middle Ages there were many liturgical manuals to oversee a complex series of daily, weekly, yearly, and occasional liturgies that, due to their number and complexity, required a trained professional to oversee.

So there was, shall we say, a lot of development. Add to that Johannes Gutenberg's invention of the movable type press in the fifteenth century, which made printing both easier and cheaper, and that technology enabled the rapid production of books and tracts. This contributed as much as anything else to the success of the Protestant Reformation in the sixteenth century.

In 1528 Thomas Cranmer was a priest and Cambridge canon law specialist when he sat in a pub one evening with a couple of friends who worked in Henry VIII's court. During that dinner Cranmer suggested that the king might have more success in resolving his little "succession problem" by seeking the opinions of scholars in the European universities rather than working through the papal court. When this was reported to Henry, he summoned Cranmer into his service and appointed Cranmer in rapid succession as ambassador to the Holy Roman Empire and archbishop of Canterbury. During his time in Germany as ambassador, Cranmer was exposed to the Lutheran Reformation and was quite impressed with it. He even married the daughter of the Reformer Andreas Osiander in the summer of 1532, something he had to conceal from King Henry, who did not permit clerical marriage. That's our guy, Thomas Cranmer. Serve the king; hide the wife and kids.

From the time he was appointed as archbishop of Canterbury in October of 1532 until Henry's death in 1547, Cranmer continued to develop his interest in Reformed thinking and worked on projects of liturgical reform in the background. From 1538 to 1539 he drafted a radical revision of the Daily Offices. While they were still in Latin, he reduced them to two, Morning and Evening, simplified them, and dramatically increased the amount of scripture, covering the entire Bible in one year. These, and a preface written for them, were the basis of what he included in the first Book of Common Prayer. In 1541, the Bible was published in English. In 1544, Cranmer received Henry's permission to produce a litany in English, a processional prayer form popular in the Middle Ages. We also have a second draft of the Daily Offices, much less radical and more reflective of Henry's conservatism during his final years. One thing that historians have made clear is how Cranmer's theology shifted as he took more interest in the eucharistic theology of Ulrich Zwingli and John Calvin, who emphasized the symbolic qualities of the bread and wine rather than viewing them as becoming Christ's body and blood in any physical sense.

Once Henry had died, Cranmer was able to act quickly. In 1548 an *Order for Holy Communion* was produced in English to be inserted into the Latin Mass just after the priest's communion. It included the confession and absolution that we know from Rite I; the Prayer of Humble Access, which restored the cup to the people with the words "and to drink his blood"; the communion of the people, which was rare in those days; the sentences of administration we know; and a final blessing. We don't know how effective it was in increasing the frequency of communion, as it wasn't in use for very long. In September 1548, Cranmer held a conference at Chertsey Abbey and in three short weeks a book was prepared that became the Book of Common Prayer in 1549. No one doubts that Cranmer was the principle architect.

With this background we can now ask the question: what is a prayer book? There are, of course, numerous answers. As a liturgical book, the Book of Common Prayer is an English-language single-volume compilation of the range of volumes previously required for parish worship.

As a reformer, Cranmer had a deep concern for teaching the scriptures to the English people, and any survey of the contents of his prayer books shows that the primary source for liturgical texts was scripture. In the Preface of that first work of revision in 1538 he wrote that

> all the whole Bible (or the greatest part thereof) should be read over once in the year, intending thereby, that the Clergy, and specially such as were Ministers of the congregation, should (by often reading and meditation of God's word) be stirred up to godliness themselves, and be more able also to exhort others by wholesome doctrine, and to confute them that were adversaries to the truth. And further, that the people (by daily hearing of holy scripture read in the Church) should continually profit more and more in the knowledge of God, and be the more inflamed with the love of his true religion.

Cranmer retained this vision of what might be called the National Monastery in his preface to the 1549 prayer book, because he envisioned everyone in the village going to the church daily for Morning and Evening Prayer, hearing the scriptures read through each year and, I love that phrase, "be the more inflamed with the love of [God's] true religion."

But it was not just Cranmer's program of public reading and hearing that taught the scriptures; an examination of his prayer books makes clear that the scriptures permeate every service. The texts of Morning and Evening Prayer are mostly scripture. The collects are filled with scriptural allusions and citations, the eucharistic prayers have scripture woven throughout, the lectionary readings are included in the book, and the entire book of Psalms is there as well. As a textbook for Bible education, the Book of Common Prayer is a reordering of Holy Scripture for the purpose of personal transformation and communal worship.

I have used the term "books" when describing his work, and Cranmer did produce a second Prayer Book in 1552, which is more clearly Reformed in perspective. Anything that smacked of superstition (anointing in baptism) or transubstantiation ("The Body of Christ" in administering communion) was removed. Language more in line with the Reformation's symbolic view of the Eucharist was introduced:

> Hear us, O merciful Father, we most humbly beseech thee; and grant that we **receiving** these thy creatures of bread and wine, according to thy Son our Saviour Jesus Christ's holy institution, in **remembrance** of his death and passion, may be

partakers of his most blessed Body and
Blood. [Bold God's]

That is what I call Cranmer's eucharistic formula:
the only way in which the bread and wine can be seen
to correlate to Christ's body and blood. In addition, and
following the practice of every other Reformer, communion was now received immediately after Christ's words
from the Last Supper. These two books represent a staged
introduction of reformed ideas, but because the founder
of the tradition produced two books, it inevitably led to
a 472-year debate of which was the better one, with more
Catholic-minded Anglicans preferring the first and more
reform-minded Anglicans preferring the second.

Shortly after the introduction of the second book,
the young king, Edward, died and was replaced with
his Roman Catholic half sister, Mary, who returned
England to Catholicism and waged a five-year persecu-
tion against Reformers, which earned her the nickname
Bloody Mary. Her final victim was Thomas Cranmer
in 1556. Mary herself died two years later, and when her
half sister Elizabeth took the throne, Elizabeth chose
the Reformed path and reinstated the 1552 prayer book
with some minor alterations intended to satisfy Catholic
concerns. This is the first but by no means the last time
that one prayer book was chosen over the other, and it
means that, in the evolution of prayer books, we have two
genetic strands of prayer books: 1549 (the more Catholic)
and 1552 (the more Reformed). Time will not allow us to
go any deeper into this story, but the short version is that
the churches of Scotland and America descended from

1549 and everyone else in the Anglican Communion descended from 1552. The Book of Common Prayer—as a living text within the Church of England and in its various namesakes across the Anglican Communion—is one of the world's finest examples of historical theology, where the Reformation concerns of the sixteenth century, the Enlightenment concerns of the eighteenth century, the Anglo-Catholic concerns of the early twentieth century, and always the practical concerns of each generation were woven into the book each time it was revised or rewritten for different worshipping communities.

Closer to our own day, the Liturgical Movement of the twentieth century drew the Western churches closer together by studying early liturgical documents and considering the liturgical needs of their own day, which by and large were those of the World War II generation. They emphasized a more active role for the laity; promoted a theology that saw Christian identity, ministry, and church governance as flowing from baptism; encouraged a return (for many of us) to the primitive practice of a weekly celebration of the Eucharist as the principle service on a Sunday; reintroduced the full run of Holy Week services; and provided worship in modern language. The list could go on and on. Nana would not recognize much of what we do today, but we are children of this movement whether we realize it or not. And this is the movement that led to an onrush of revised prayer books in the second half of the twentieth and first years of the twenty-first centuries. Our own 1979 Book of Common Prayer is an early example of a Liturgical Movement revision, and all Anglican revisions from this time represent a third genetic strand of the Book of Common Prayer, Liturgical Movement prayer books. These were the first books that were not primarily the texts of Thomas Cranmer, and perhaps that huge change helps explain why it was challenging to introduce, perhaps it explains why so many still do not understand the central baptismal theology of the book, and perhaps it explains why, forty plus years later, it is worrying for many to consider going into a period of revision again. Remember that groan in Philadelphia?

Finally, and perhaps for our purposes most importantly, the Book(s) of Common Prayer, in all their many forms and editions, have been the Anglican flesh and blood on the skeleton of the biblical ordo of Christian worship; retaining the word/prayer ordo in the Daily Offices, restoring the word/bath/meal ordo of Christian initiation, and restoring the word/meal ordo as the central act of Sunday worship. I don't think it is possible to overestimate the importance of the prayer book for our identity as Anglicans and our theology as Catholic, Reformed, Enlightenment and Liturgical Movement Christians. We are no one thing, we Episcopalians. Layers have accumulated over time because one of our chief characteristics, dating back to the founder of the tradition Thomas Cranmer himself, is that as we move forward we always try to bring the central things with us. That is the common thread. Most traditions do that in some form, but I don't know of anyone who attempts to locate the central things in one place to the extent that we have. This is what makes us Anglicans, this is what makes revision so difficult for us, and this is what makes revision so important for our life as a Christian church in a changing world with a mission to those who are lost.

CHAPTER EIGHT

Elements of an Anglican Liturgical Theology

New Creation I

IN THE FALL of 2018, I knew that a friend had nominated me to the Task Force on Liturgical and Prayer Book Revision. I appreciated the vote of confidence but was still surprised when I received the email informing me of my appointment. The composition of the task force was intended to be as diverse as possible. I know that that is harder to do than it sounds, but the task force is nonetheless heavily weighted towards white men. There are only seven women, in part because bishops make up one-third of the total group and only one of the bishops is female. Those who do not trace their ancestry back to Europe are also underrepresented, and at the time of appointment there were no deacons. There are several members from the LGBTQ community.

The first task force meeting was fine. Thirty people, all of whom are interested in liturgy, is my idea of a good time. I had never worked on a national body before and was interested in how it would work and whether I could find my voice in it. What I remember of the first couple of days was that we had honest conversations about our understandings of what Resolution A068 intended and our level of consensus regarding what our work entailed. We had large-group discussions and small-group discussions and the point eventually arrived when it was time to identify the subcommittees that would take up our time in between group meetings. We agreed on four subcommittees:

> Subcommittee 1: **Seek, Receive, and Review**: The Rt. Rev. Mary Glasspool, The Rt. Rev. Matthew A. Gunter, The Rev. Dr. Ruth Meyers, The Rev. Dr. Matthew S.C. Olver, The Rt. Rev. Brian Thom.

> Subcommittee 2: **Communications**: Mr. Christopher Decatur, The Rev. Matthew Mead, Ms. Kathleen Moore, The Rev. Zack Nyein.

> Subcommittee 3: **Constitution and Canons Review**: Dr. Mark

Ardrey-Graves, The Rev. Paul Fromburg,
Ms. Joan Geiszler-Ludlum, The Rt.
Rev. Wendell Gibbs, Lcdo. Adrián
Linares-Palacios, Mr. James Scott.

Subcommittee 4: **Liturgical Revision
and Creation:** Mr. Ron Braman,
The Very Rev. Samuel G. Candler,
Mr. Craig Dressler, Sister Ellen Francis,
OSH, The Rev. Deon Johnson,
The Rev. Dr. Kevin Moroney, The
Rev. Dr. Cameron Partridge, The
Rev. Dr. Nina Ranadive Pooley,
The Rev. Dr. Lauren Winner.

I am on the fourth subcommittee and I was excited about that because I have been working on concerns related to prayer book revision since my doctorate in Dublin. I don't recall much of the content of that first subcommittee meeting in Maryland but I do remember two things: I started to find my voice and I was surprised that the voice I was finding sounded more conservative. That was surprising to me because, since this conversation began following General Convention 2015, I am one of the few liturgists I know who fully supported revision. I would talk about how many Anglican provinces have gone on to revise again since their first round in the '70s or '80s. I would comment that most of the arguments I heard against prayer book revision sounded fear-based to me, often driven by a distrust over who would be making the decisions (remember power?), and how fear-based decisions are rarely our best ones. I would argue that the best way to further the work of the 1979 prayer book would be to articulate more clearly its theology of baptism while addressing those things left undone such as those to do with language and creation theology. I liked to use the word "refinement" while my mentor Neil Alexander liked to use the phrase "fine tuning," but we seemed to share a similar and, some might say, naive opinion that a thoughtful but not radical revision of the prayer book would be something that the Episcopal Church can handle. I'm sure that I was saying those kinds of things at the meeting but instead of sounding progressive as it usually did, I walked away from that first meeting feeling more conservative than I usually do.

Over the course of the next six months our subcommittee had a little trouble finding traction. During a January 2019 Zoom meeting I agreed to write a paper on what we might revise if we do revise and after several months of struggling to find focus, rather like a group version of finding our voice, that paper became the agenda for our online discussions. I got the idea for the paper from a prayer book we have in our special collections in the library here at General Seminary: the personal prayer book of William Reed Huntington, best known as the author of the Chicago Lambeth Quadrilateral. Less known is that his calls for prayer book revision eventually led to the 1892 prayer book. As a method for organizing his thoughts, he went through his own prayer book and wrote in the margins what he would change if he could change it. I liked the concept he used, so I bought a new large print prayer book and did the same thing: page by page, I wrote in everything I would do if I could do it. I then transcribed it into a paper for our subcommittee to discuss. By this time we had also divided into two sub-subcommittees, one focused purely on prayer book revision while the other one focused on liturgical creation and, more specifically, inclusive and expansive language. I presented my original paper in May and reduced it to a two-page document, which became the basis for our discussions. If you have interest, each paper is presented here, in appendix A and B.

To my way of thinking, the fulcrum on which everything else rests is the resolution's apparent guarantee of the continued use of the 1979 prayer book without specifying for how long. I raised this in a number of meetings and suggested that we could both revise the prayer book and allow its continued use, but comments made in response were that the Episcopal Church has always been a one-book church and that should continue. My concern about that perspective is that I have had a lot of conversations with people who will be extremely distressed if our current prayer book is taken away from them. I have also had a lot of conversations with people who feel like we are late catching up on issues of language. We were now having really good conversations as a committee, but the win/win we were looking for was not emerging.

As we began to look ahead to our next task force gathering in Atlanta on October 22 to 25, 2019, the chair of our subcommittee, Deon Johnson, produced a document that attempted to weave together all the concerns expressed regarding possible revision. The other sub-subcommittee in our group began working on a document for principles for inclusive language, so we felt like between the two papers we would have some good contributions to make in Atlanta.

What I remember about the opening of that October meeting is that we reintroduced ourselves by processing our different perspectives about our task, including the reality that not everyone on the task force wanted to revise the prayer book. The conversation was gracious and respectful but clearly without consensus. I went straight to bed.

The next thing I knew was when I woke up at four the next morning. There was a thought in my head; a kind of unformed idea that I can't really describe, an attempt to synthesize everything I heard in the conversation the evening before. I spit it out into a Word doc and then fiddled with it for a while and it came out something like this:

> In light of the fact that Resolution A068 calls us to "memorialize" the 1979 BCP, calls us to revise the BCP and create new liturgies, and calls us to use emerging technologies in this new era of revision, one possibility is for us to:
>
> 1. Recommend that the primary platform for our revision be digital and online, allowing us to authorize more material than is possible within the

limits of a printed book (with printed books remaining as an option);

2. That this new revision be titled *Common Prayer* or something similar that sets it within the BCP tradition;

3. That the 1979 BCP be the first material included in this work;

4. That revised liturgies that are consistent with the Trinitarian, Baptismal, and Eucharistic theology of the 1979 BCP, reflect the mandates in A068 regarding inclusive and expansive language, creation care, etc., and that are passed by two consecutive General Conventions, be part of this *Common Prayer* and considered fully authorized liturgies in the Episcopal Church.

This does not exclude the possibility of having "Alternative" liturgies to supplement *Common Prayer*, passed by one General Convention, as was passed on a first reading in 2018.

Our subcommittee worked on it in our morning meeting and then presented the refined version to the task force that afternoon. The subcommittee version is:

Common Prayer
Worship in the Episcopal Church

A Proposal by the Task Force for Liturgical and Prayer Book Revision
10/24/2019

Resolution A068 calls us to memorialize the 1979 BCP, create new liturgies, and use emerging technologies. Thus we propose the following:

1. That the 1979 BCP is the foundation and model for common prayer and liturgical development in the Episcopal Church.

2. That the 1979 BCP is maintained as an authorized text within a growing set of authorized liturgical materials for common prayer.

3. That the primary platform for our authorized liturgies be digital and online—organized according to the shape of the 1979 BCP—thus allowing for the authorization of more material than is possible within the limits of a printed book (with printed books remaining as an option).

4. That this new set of authorized liturgies be titled *Common Prayer: Worship in the Episcopal Church*, or something similar that sets it within the BCP tradition.

5. That authorized liturgies will be consistent with the Trinitarian, Baptismal, and Eucharistic theology of the 1979 BCP; and will be consonant with the directives of the General Convention with respect to liturgical language, inclusive and expansive language, and creation care; and will honor the Church's increasing diversity.

6. That we continue the requirement of approval by two consecutive General Conventions for authorized rites included in *Common Prayer: Worship in the Episcopal Church*, and that we encourage the further development of alternative rites for use.

It went before the task force with a good discussion. I tried to explain it as best I could but I hadn't known it much longer than anyone else had, so I was thinking on my feet. After thirty minutes or so, the task force unanimously voted that this idea would be part of what we would present to General Convention in 2021 as our recommendation for how we might move forward. As I got to know this proposal, I could see how strands from everything that had ever formed me were woven into it, the central one being that everyone should be respected enough to see that their needs are met if there is any way to meet them. Oddly enough, I had to leave the meeting first thing the next morning, one day early. The meeting would continue with other good work being done but back at General we were dedicating the portrait of H. Boone Porter, in whose chair I sat, and I had to be there. So as fast as the idea came, I had to go, and once again I sat on a plane feeling my ancestors and my dead parents surging up inside of me. I love that feeling and it only happens every so often.

CHAPTER NINE

Elements of an Anglican Liturgical Theology

New Creation II

I'VE NOW HAD some time to live with this idea and consider why I think it is the right way forward. You should also know that at that same meeting of the task force we made the decision to make public all of our approved documents, as soon as translations were completed, so Episcopalians who cared about the topic would not only know what we are doing in this and other proposals but that they could participate by suggesting edits to our work. Brilliant. You can see this proposal and others at www.episcopalcommonprayer.org.

I have spent a lot of time since that first resolution was passed in 2015 talking with a wide range of folks; through those conversations, I have gained a sense of what I see as the major bodies of opinion about prayer book and liturgical revision as we look ahead. Because we joke that there are two types of people in the world, let us say there are those who oppose prayer book revision and those who favor it. Among those who oppose revision I have met four "sub-types": those for whom revision, after having lived through the introduction of the 1979 prayer book, is untenable; those for whom the cost of a new prayer book cannot be justified though new liturgical options are of interest; those for whom the battle just isn't worth fighting; and those who see our need to "live into the 1979 book more fully" to be more compelling than the need for a new book.

Those who favor prayer book revision also can be understood as falling into four "sub-types": those for whom the revisions can be understood as minor "tweaks"; those for whom revision—especially around issues of language—is long overdue; those who wish to expand the range of our liturgical and ritual life; and those who suggest that the lead set by the Church of England, where the 1662 Book of Common Prayer is still the official volume and multiple volumes of additional liturgical material are available (and far more widely used), may be the way forward.

There is only one other demographic I can identify, which I am told is actually the largest. This is the "we really don't care" crowd—good and faithful members of our parishes who attend and pledge and come to coffee hour but who don't know who their bishop is, have no idea what a province is, and don't know what the prayer book is because they are handed a full text bulletin when they walk through our red doors.

My most basic concern is that we have addressed issues in the last fifty years that simply had to be dealt with and that did not allow for half measures. We had to either approve women's ordination or not. We had to be leaders in the Liturgical Movement and revise the American prayer book in line with its principles or not. We had to either approve ordination for those in the LGBTQ community or not. We had to either approve marriage equality or not. We could not simply ignore everything that was going on around us, but there has been a lot of pain in this body and for lots of complicated reasons we have lost a lot of people. So, in light of that, it is my view that we do not have to, cannot afford to, and probably should not want to see prayer book revision as another church-splitting vote. I hope that it is time for us to cherish each other enough in the Episcopal Church to allow the few of us who are left to live in peace. This proposal is an attempt to enable us to do just that. It requires one conceptual shift from book to digital platform (with both printing and downloading opportunities), and it requires those on either side of the revision debate to accept the provision made for the other side. If those two things can be accomplished then we have something that is inclusive enough and with wide enough arms to keep both what is good about our past while simultaneously embracing the new. No one has to use what they do not want to, provision will be made in line with the mandates of the resolution regarding theology, language, enculturation, and creation care, and limits for inclusion will be determined by the General Convention.

Allow me to comment on the six points of the proposal by taking two at a time:

1. That the 1979 BCP is the foundation and model for common prayer and liturgical development in the Episcopal Church.

2. That the 1979 BCP is maintained as an authorized text within a growing set of authorized liturgical materials for common prayer.

The sub-subcommittee considerably strengthened my original language regarding the 1979 prayer book. I originally had it as the fourth point and identified it as the first deposit into this new library of fully authorized rites. As a group we felt that there is a lot of anxiety coming from those who seek to retain the BCP, so we moved it to the top and expanded it into two points, assuring that any new work would remain in the trajectory of the 1979 book and defining what it means to "memorialize" the BCP by making it perpetually available within a "growing set" of authorized material. It may run out of steam someday but it will do so on its own, not because anyone forced it.

Mindful of the liturgical theology presented in this book, the proposal would carry forward the 1979 prayer book's limited creation theology, exclusive language for people in certain places, and male domination in language for God throughout. This is a serious shortcoming for some and it is where I would ask those most deeply concerned about these issues to consider three points: The 1979 prayer book is a strong book biblically and theologically. We have learned and grown since then but it is still a good prayer book, important historically and an excellent example of Liturgical Movement theology. It is not a bad place to start. Second, issues of inclusive and expansive language do not require the exclusion of traditional language but can build from it. The word "expand" can be seen as implying expansion from the traditional language, thus allowing for some continued use. Third, we do not have an army to remove the 1979 prayer books from the pews of churches who wish to retain it, so it is better to permit than fail at implementation and create more hurt. Whatever its short comings, it is historically and theologically important enough to us that continuing its authorization is worth consideration.

3. That the primary platform for our authorized liturgies be digital and online—organized according to the shape of the 1979 BCP—thus allowing for the authorization of more material than is possible within the limits of a printed book (with printed books remaining as an option).

4. That this new set of authorized liturgies be titled *Common Prayer: Worship in the Episcopal Church*, or something similar that sets it within the BCP tradition.

I originally placed these clauses at the opening of the document because they articulate the conceptual change that make this growing set possible. When Johannes Gutenburg invented movable type in the fifteenth century, book production as we know it was born and the millennia-old technology of hand-copied books gradually faded away. The reformers took that technology and disseminated their concerns through the rapid printing of pamphlets and books. Print is with us still and is not going away, though there are limits to it. If our liturgical resources are limited to 1001 pages (the size of the current prayer book), then some are going to win and some are going to lose and some of those who lose are going to walk. By accepting a conceptual change of media platform from book to digital, there will be enough room for almost everyone. At a minimum this would mean that we can expand our concerns in both directions to include the 1979 prayer book, as previously stated, along with implementing mandates regarding inclusive language, expansive language, enculturation, and creation theology in revised and new liturgies.

The insertion of the phrase "organized according to the shape of the 1979 BCP" is another way to memorialize our current book while taking a step to ensure that the new concept looks like a single creation instead of the 1979 prayer book linked to other materials that remain separate while within the whole. All Daily Office services will appear as a group. All baptismal rites will appear as a group. All eucharistic liturgies will appear as a group. It emphasizes that *Common Prayer*, or whatever it may ultimately be named, is seen as one work rather than many.

The suggested title is simply a reflection of the new platform: we take the Book of Common Prayer, remove *The Book of* because we are not conceptually talking about a book anymore, and are left with *Common Prayer.* Technological advancement may have given us what we desperately need: the ability to open our liturgical arms wide enough so that all of our members are within the reach of a saving embrace.

I also want to say that this proposal is not a renunciation of books. Studies have shown that book sales are ticking back up again. While the details will obviously have to be worked out, there can be any number of ways to publish this "growing set of authorized liturgical materials."

> 5. That authorized liturgies will be consistent with the Trinitarian, Baptismal, and Eucharistic theology of the 1979 BCP; and will be consonant with the directives of the General Convention with respect to liturgical language, inclusive and expansive language, and creation care; and will honor the Church's increasing diversity.

> 6. That we continue the requirement of approval by two consecutive General Conventions for authorized rites included in *Common Prayer: Worship in the Episcopal Church*, and that we encourage the further development of alternative rites for use.

The final two clauses simply refine the language of the original proposal and add what was a concluding comment on the original to make a sixth point here. On the one hand, number five is a continuation of number one, where the 1979 BCP is described as "the foundation and model for common prayer and liturgical development." That foundation is here specified as the "Trinitarian, Baptismal and Eucharistic theology" of the book, which is itself an allusion to clauses 4 and 5 of Resolution A068. On the other hand, clause 5 is the theological heart of the proposal. We stay grounded within the "orthodox" Christian faith while seeing that faith expressed in concerns about theological and liturgical language. It is not a challenge or a weakening of orthodoxy but essential to it. To those who do not agree with this point and see the 1979 prayer book as the one guarantor of Christian orthodoxy, then we remind everyone that the breadth of this proposal means that no one has to use rites that they do not want to use. It only requires the allowance of theological room for the other.

The final clause is similarly an extension of point one of the proposal as an attempt to provide the necessary limits on this "growing set of authorized liturgical materials." There is a real concern that broadening our current one-book system could open the door to liturgical chaos. I'm afraid that the bad news is that we already have a fair amount of liturgical chaos. The better news is that this is not new and liturgical history can provide an answer. Horton Davies wrote in his 1930s classic, *Worship and Theology in England,* that "it is hardly possible to exaggerate the ceremonial chaos in the early years of the 20th century." A royal commission published a report in 1906 stating that the laws of worship were too narrow, and that steps should be taken to broaden them. In other words, we have not dealt with liturgical chaos by nipping it in the bud and stamping it out, and when we have tried that we have failed miserably. Instead the task force has broadened what the rubrics allow in order to get our arms around it and place liturgical freedom within appropriate authority. The first thing that *Common Prayer* proposes to do by maintaining an authorization process that requires approval at two consecutive General Conventions is to ensure that such a thing as "common prayer" still exists. It may not be a single book anymore, but only that which represents the highest level of theological and liturgical consensus in the Episcopal Church will be able to make it through the rigorous current process of authorization. This is not an "anything goes" proposal. The second thing it does is encourage "the further development of alternative rites for use," which acknowledges that there may be liturgies that meet particular needs but may not rise to that highest level of consensus. Considerable freedom under appropriate authority. No chaos (or at least limits on it). Room for more than a book can contain.

In class I like to remind my students that while we are familiar with the scripture "There is no Jew or Greek, there is no slave or free, there is no longer male and female," we are less aware that the radical equality expressed in that passage is set within the context of baptism:

> As many of you as were baptized into
> Christ have clothed yourselves with
> Christ. There is no longer Jew or Greek,
> there is no longer slave or free, there is
> no longer male and female; for all of
> you are one in Christ Jesus. (Galatians
> 3:27–28)

We are always striving to live into what it means to be the children of God in Christ. I agree with those who say that we have never fully lived into the vision and theology of the 1979 prayer book. We are striving to live into what it means to be the baptized just as we citizens of the United States are striving to live into what it means when our Declaration of Independence says that we are all created equal. In our context, it is not so much about a book as it is about Common Prayer for the entire Episcopal Church. It is a new attempt at being a new creation. If it is not the Kingdom of God come in its fullness it may be a step in that direction, and one we can all take together. Please God make it so.

At its final meeting in November 2020, the task force reviewed the final report for General Convention. The "Common Prayer" proposal would require an amendment to Article X of the Constitution and Canons in order for it to become the liturgical pathway for the Episcopal Church. Several options regarding how to do that were discussed, but the one that was approved came from the Rev. Matthew Mead, secretary to the task force, who proposed the following:

> The Book of Common Prayer is
> understood to be those liturgical forms
> authorized by the General Convention
> as provided for in Section 2 of this
> article.

This proposal retains the title "Book of Common Prayer" but redefines it as anything that General Convention approves at two consecutive conventions. Thus, "book" is to be understood as authorized liturgical forms and not always to be taken literally. The proposal and amendment will need to go together, and if they do, then we will have a uniquely American model of how to move forward in the prayer book tradition.

CHAPTER TEN

One Soul's Tale

Enough Already

ONE MORE STORY. I grew up with pets and, like a lot of us who do, I carry this soft spot in my heart that is the belief that pets are better than people, really. No disrespect to those humans who have journeyed with me all these years, but my best friend as a child was my dog Katie. She was wonderful beyond words and, as in many families who never displayed emotion, she was the unspoken but clearly authorized dispenser and recipient of love. She was adorable and I carry her with me always, but this is not her story.

One of the raps against clergy is that we work days, nights, and weekends, and that is often true, so as a priest I did not have a lot of spare time and in the early years of my ministry, I did not have as many pets as I did as a kid. But every so often I liked to hear myself say, "I'm thinkin' of gettin' a dog," just because I liked to hear myself say it. Every six months or so. No intention of actually doing it, mind you. During my Dublin years, I was having lunch with a student one day and I was due for saying it so I did and that was that. Duty done for another six months. "I'm thinkin' of gettin' a dog. Check, please." What I didn't expect is that when I arrived home an hour or so later there was a message from the student on the machine: "Kevin, we got you a dog!" Ahem. Return call. Steadily backpedal. Don't care for collies. Oh, not that kind of collie. What kind then? A border collie. Oh, I like those. Very smart. Okay I'll go look, but I really don't think . . .

You know what happened. I got to the vet who was looking for homes for a brother and sister who were pulled out of a river in a garbage bag because someone was walking over the bridge, saw the bag wiggling in the water, went down and pulled them out, and brought them to the vet. I was told at the desk that the boy had been taken but the girl was still in the back, which was fine because I had only ever had female dogs. Wait, did I just say that? Uh oh. The vet took me back and there, sitting in the corner trembling, was the dog who stole my heart. Mostly black with a discernable chestnut hue and a bright white chest. I named her "Lucy in the Sky with Diamonds" because her predecessor many years earlier was "Penny Lane" and I prefer Lennon anyway, by a lot.

I put her in the new retractable-roof Volkswagen I had bought for my fortieth birthday, got up on the road, and Lucy began our life together by puking all over my new cloth seats during the entire forty-minute drive home. That's my kind of girl. Anxious to the bone. It was Maundy Thursday, 2002. She became the college dog and she knew every dorm room that housed treats. When I was serving at St. John's, Dublin, she was the parish dog. I'd keep her in the sacristy but during one Mass I went down for my genuflection and there she was sticking her cold nose in my worshipful face. She was uncontainable in those early years. Lucy would chase a tennis ball all day and all night. One time she ran into a soccer game, stole the ball from an unsuspecting player, and no one could catch her until I eventually used what later came to be called my "Dad voice," which stopped her in her tracks. Those years were a lot of fun and she had a whole gang of other dogs in Dublin to play with.

When I came home to the States, I brought her with me and when the people at JFK wheeled her out to baggage claim in her crate and she saw me, she rolled the thing over. She became a full-time parish dog. And the neighborhood dog. Most of my early friends in Pennsylvania were other people who walked their dogs at the same time I did. I'm a bit ritualistic. People I never knew would walk up to me and say "You're the guy with the dog. Every day I know if I'm late for my train or not depending on where I pass you on the sidewalk." When I changed parishes and the nursery school said that some of the kids were scared of her and said I needed to stop bringing her I did what anyone would do; I moved my office to the other side of the building. It was either that or shut down the nursery school.

By the time we moved to New York, Lucy was fifteen years old and starting to show signs of aging. When I took her for her annual checkup about nine months after we moved to New York, the vet heard something funny when he checked her heart. We discovered that she had a significantly enlarged heart and that there was nothing to do but use medicine to try and keep her comfortable. She was with us for a couple more weeks.

That is not the story I want to tell you, however: you just need to know that background in order to understand the larger story. That, and one other thing: the only New York City I like is the one I discovered riding my bike at six o'clock in the morning. It is quiet. The sidewalks and streets are mostly empty. You can hear yourself think. The sky brightens in the east, bringing the hopeful promise of a new day, which is at least part of the reason I started doing this in the first place. That and I love the feeling of wind in my face. Riding has been an integral piece of my personal resurrection. And you know what happens when you open up emotional space in your life . . .

On the way back from a morning ride one day, I stopped at the light at 7th Avenue and 21st Street. I glanced to the left and froze at the sight of the vet office where I had said goodbye to Lucy. It had been two and a half years but I burst into tears and had a good old cry for my beloved Lucy. It's a bit surreal sitting on your bike and sobbing all by yourself on a quiet New York street that is usually all noise and people. The moment came and I let it come. The moment passed and I let it pass. Emotions can hit you like a wave and then go back out to sea; thank God. It took me years to learn that. I pulled my left pedal back the way I do, pushed forward and headed for home and children.

I have learned that grief is not just about dealing with loss. It is also about allowing the weight and burden of deep, deep sadness to purge itself from our system so we can keep the good and carry on. The seismic changes that have happened to the world, to the United States, to the Church, and specifically, for you and me, dear reader, to the Episcopal Church have encompassed a lot of life with no small amount of grief. Who's in, who's out, and why. Managing the decline. I have heard conservatives speak uncharitably about liberals and I have heard liberals say good riddance to those who felt that they had to leave. But perhaps we have hurt enough and lost enough to see this moment as an opportunity to pick up the good and walk together into our future.

A few years back, the Pennsylvania Supreme Court surprised a lot of us by ruling in favor of same-sex marriage, but because there was a Republican in the governor's office we assumed that it would be challenged. Imagine my surprise a few days later when Governor Corbett announced that he would not challenge the ruling— making marriage equality the law in just a couple of days.

A few weeks later I was walking from my car to my office with my daughter Maggie, who was about six at the time. As we walked, Maggie asked, "Daddy, do I have to marry a boy?"

Mindful of our recent legal changes I thought carefully about my answer and said something I never could have said before: "Sweetie, you can marry whoever you want." That felt right.

Maggie agreed: "Good, because the kids on the playground said I have to marry a boy and I don't want to."

"Sweetie, no one can tell you who to love; you marry whoever you want."

Our common prayer is a big part of what is good about us; I would say it is our greatest contribution to the larger Church. And a big part of what makes it great is how each generation discerns how to carry forward the good while making room for change that responds to our current needs. It can be a painful process, but it is good. It is who we are as members of creation, as children of the Bible, as people who fill the ordo with the prayer book, and as God's new creation, world without end. Amen.

Appendix A

Proposals for the Revision
of the 1979 Book of Common Prayer

The Rev. Canon Dr. Kevin J. Moroney

General Considerations

1. *Table of Contents.* For a printed prayer book, the section at the front is where a non-specialist is likely to look first. Perhaps we could move the calendar to the back with the lectionaries, and have a section for "Daily Prayer for Individuals, Households and Congregations" that can include short prayer offices, a section of prayers like what we now have towards the back of the book, and the Daily Offices. Pew research has shown that, while Sunday attendance has declined, personal prayer has increased, and we can provide resources for that need.

2. *Inclusive and Expansive Language.* We will need a uniform policy on how to implement inclusive and

expansive language. Resolution A068 states that our liturgical revision will "utilize inclusive and expansive language and imagery for humanity and divinity." My own view on how to implement this principle will depend on how long the 1979 rites remain available in their current form. If they will be available perpetually, I can see applying inclusive and expansive language principles throughout our revision work. If the '79 rites will only be available until a full revision is completed, then I would suggest a more nuanced implementation of inclusive/expansive language. In Rite I, I suggest limiting our revision work in this area to language related to humanity and reducing the number of times God is referred to as "Father. " (See work from 2016.) In Rite II, I suggest building from the resolution passed at General Convention in 2018 regarding inclusive/expansive language changes in our Rite II Eucharist and strive to balance our language but keep the flow and feel of the prayers unchanged. These are both pastoral and political considerations for those who do not seek dramatic changes to the current rites. New additions to the prayer book will be fully inclusive/expansive, building off of EOW and working with new liturgies that are produced.

3. *Creation Theology.* Resolution A068 states that "our liturgical revision shall incorporate and express understanding, appreciation, and care of God's creation . . . " The catechism of the prayer book should begin with a section on creation theology, rather than starting with human nature, as it now does. Also, any

language in eucharistic prayers that describe us as "rulers" of creation should be removed and replaced with a more suitable word. I am not convinced that "steward" is the best word either. Collects that include themes for the four seasons could be included in the Daily Offices or section of prayers.

4. It would be preferable to have rubrics in red.

5. We need a new preface that gives background for the '79 prayer book (which inexplicably provided no new preface) as well as an explanation for this current era of revision.

Concerning the Service of the Church

1. If the creative freedom described in A068 is to continue, it may need to be described here.

Calendar

1. As stated above, the calendar can be moved to the back of the book with the lectionaries. Its use is technical and is not useful to most people.

2. Lesser Feasts should not be listed because that list changes at every General Convention.

The Daily Offices

1. Should the term "Presider" be substituted for "Officiant" as it is for "Celebrant" in the Eucharist, or will it be used in exclusive reference to the Eucharist?

2. For the scripture citations at the beginning, a more modern translation could help with inclusive language issues.

3. The exhortation prior to the confession is one place where inclusive language work needs to be done.

4. For the Invitatory and Canticles, there are more recent versions that should help with inclusive language.

5. Antiphons: are they used? In my experience they are more confusing than enriching. The rubric, which now says that they may be sung or said "with" the invitatory psalm, might clarify the confusion by reading "before and after," unless we want a kind of freedom that retains the confusion.

6. Canticles: Rite I vs. Rite II. Perhaps leave Rite I alone while using more recent versions in Rite II. Perhaps add some from EOW I such as "The Song of Wisdom." Bringing in new canticles may require us to take out a few existing ones. Update "Suggested Canticles" on pages 144–145.

7. Collects: Here is where we can look at language relating to God. Keep "Father" language to a minimum while bringing in other biblical language.

8. The General Thanksgiving: In Rite I, change "men" to "whom you have made" from Rite II.

9. Daily Devotions for Individuals and Families could be moved to the front for easy access as per earlier comments.

10. Additional Directions: Should Ghost be changed to Spirit throughout as was done in the Irish BCP of 2004?

11. Is the full Venite on page 146 used?

Litany

Time for a Rite II Litany (see Common Worship and C of I, 2004).

Collects

1. Bring back all four "Stir up" Collects for Advent as the Lutherans have done?

2. Collects are one place where we can work on our language about God. With that said, only 18 of 149 collects address God as Father.

3. What is the life span of the RCL? If our lectionary is stable, it would be good to more fully correlate the themes of our collects to the lectionary.

Proper Liturgies for Special Days

1. For congregations who do not have the clergy coverage or people to celebrate each of these rites, perhaps Palm Sunday could accommodate parts of Maundy Thursday as it has Good Friday through the reading of the Passion. Such a liturgy would include:

    a. Liturgy of the Palms with procession

b. Liturgy of the Word with Maundy Thursday readings

c. Foot washing ceremony.

d. Creed, prayers (or Prayer D), confession

e. Eucharist

f. Stripping of the altar

g. Reading of the Passion

h. Depart in silence

2. With a meditation rather than a full sermon this alternative takes no more time than usual.

3. For congregations that cannot celebrate the vigil, perhaps the lighting of the Easter fire/Paschal candle and procession into the church leading to the Easter Acclamation could precede the first Eucharist on Easter morning. The renewal of baptismal vows could also be used.

4. Such permission could be described at the beginning of the section under the heading "Concerning the Services."

5. In the Maundy Thursday service, perhaps include the instructions from *The Book of Occasional Services*.

Holy Baptism

1. *Concerning the Service*: In the first paragraph I recommend the addition of something like "All the baptized are welcome to receive the Eucharist," although, given our discernment around

communion prior to baptism, it may be best to leave it as is. I would also add a note to the effect that "It is customary to refrain from baptisms during Lent and to prepare to hold them at the Easter Vigil or during Eastertide."

2. I would add two more expansive opening acclamations that are more inclusive/expansive, and I would use "The Grace" as one of them.

3. In the section beginning "There is one Body and one Spirit," I might add an additional couplet from Galatians 3:

   a. As many of you as [are] baptized into
      Christ have clothed yourselves with
      Christ;

   b. There is no longer Jew or Greek,
      there is no longer slave or free,
      there is no longer male and female;
      [we] are all one in Christ.

4. I have a question about the flow of the rite, specifically concerning whether the five questions of the "Covenant" should follow the baptism as the response to Grace. If changes are made, we would have to make sure that they work equally well during the Easter Vigil and Confirmation.

5. I find that it is effective to pour the water into the font *during* the prayer over the water, providing some sense of "living" water. Perhaps the note in "Additional Directions" could be amended to allow this.

6. There is a tension in the rite related to the episcopal/presbyteral prayer for the gifts of the Spirit and anointing in baptism and the episcopal prayer for the power of the Spirit and laying on of hands under the title of "At Confirmation, Reception, or Reaffirmation" that immediately follows it. We arguably have two forms of confirmation but only one bearing the title.

7. I suggest putting a rubric about presenting a baptismal candle in the rite itself.

The Holy Eucharist

1. Rite I: Does anyone use the Exhortation?

2. The formatting for the traditional Decalogue is problematic, requiring too many page changes for such a short rite.

3. Additional acclamations should match other services.

4. I do not consider the Kyrie or Trisagion appropriate *after* the absolution. They should precede the confession or the absolution. While the Gloria would be appropriate after the absolution, I would omit it as an option here.

5. In *Concerning the Celebration*, second paragraph, "presider" should replace "principal celebrant" and should replace "celebrant" throughout our revisions.

6. The rubric before the Collect for Purity could say *The [Presider] says this or another appropriate gathering prayer.*

7. As stated before, I favor a "lighter" implementation of inclusive/expansive language in Rite I, but in the Gloria I would change "men" to something like "all."

8. We might consider making some portions of the liturgy uniform between Rites I and II. The Gospel responses are one area to consider, the Creed another, the sursum corda another.

9. Does anyone use the first-person Creed?

10. In the Rite I Prayers of the People a rubric permits a congregational response. I recommend putting a response in the text.

11. In the Confession, I would delete the word "men."

12. The Absolution and Comfortable Words need some inclusive language work while maintaining the cadences of the language.

13. I would leave Prayer I alone for the most part, while reducing "Father" language.

14. In the Prayer of Humble Access, I would change "property" to "nature."

15. Similar to Prayer I, I would reduce the "Father" language in Prayer II.

16. I would do the same with Rite II as I recommended for Rite I in points 3–6.

17. Use the newer Gloria that does not make use of the male pronoun for God.

18. General Convention passed a resolution in the 1990s stating that any new prayer book would take out the *filioque* clause. As is true with the Gloria, there is a newer Creed we can use.

19. In Prayers of the People, the six forms referred to on page 383 have grown so tired. Perhaps we could include new forms, including seasonal forms, and produce a book of prayer forms that can be used. There are also books that have forms tied to the RCL, which pull a thematic thread through the liturgy better than our current forms.

20. Regarding our existing eucharistic prayers we need a policy on what level of revision they should undergo. If they will remain available in their current form we can produce more thoroughly revised versions. If our work will replace them I would favor a lighter revision for those who are not looking for major change. General Convention did pass a resolution that provided inclusive language options for certain sections. They could be implemented. More creation theology could be included. Will we continue to include the rubric requiring the Presider to touch the bread and the cup?

21. In Prayers C and D, we should find words other than "ruler" and "rule" to describe our relationship to creation.

22. In Prayer C, the listing of the Patriarchs has been a problem for years, but I am not convinced that elongating the phrase with women does anything for the prayer (although I fully support gender balance in our praying). For that matter, I don't see the point of going back to the Hebrew Covenant this late in the prayer—a section of the prayer that is really for fruitful reception. I would simply strike the reference to patriarchs. Something like "Redeeming God, open our eyes . . ."

23. The decision regarding whether we continue to use a book, revise electronic supplements to a book, or opt solely for digital materials, will also impact how many eucharistic prayers we can authorize. Material from *Enriching Our Worship* should also be reviewed and considered for inclusion. This, I believe, is a better place to work on gender balance.

24. Regarding formatting, every eucharistic prayer should continue through to the dismissal. It would not take up much space but would make for easier use.

25. The ending rites are sometimes referred to as "The Sending." I would recommend strengthening our "sending" language, both by including the short rite for Lay Eucharistic Ministers and including more missional language in our post-communion prayers.

26. "An Order for Celebrating the Holy Eucharist" should be updated, either using the EOW version or new work.

27. *The Book of Occasional Services* has a section on seasonal blessings. Should the "Additional Directions" section include a reference to BOS for either this reason or any other resource that is available there?

Confirmation

1. It is time to clarify the relationship between baptism and confirmation. One tool other Provinces have used is a "Pastoral Introduction" that explains the rites. We could use such a method throughout a new prayer book, but I raise it here because, in this case, we could provide a pastoral and theological explanation of confirmation as a public affirmation of one's baptism. With that said, I take issue with the use of the word "mature." I know it was introduced to provide some measuring tool, but I believe it has been more problematic than helpful. The 1662 prayer book included a rubric saying that anyone who was "ready and desirous" to be confirmed could receive communion and, while admission to communion is a different issue, I prefer language like that because it is easier to discern what a person desires than it is to discern if they are mature enough in our estimation. At a minimum, those who had vows taken for them at baptism should affirm those vows publically when they are ready, and while maturity sometimes contributes to readiness, so does active faith.

2. In the Presentation, I would duplicate the renunciations and reaffirmations from baptism so the connection is clearer.

3. In baptism, the post-baptismal prayer for the gifts of the Spirit and anointing parallels the laying on of hands and prayer for the Spirit here. What is the relationship between the two?

Marriage

1. General Convention has passed two gender-neutral marriage rites. At least one should be included in a revised prayer book. At a minimum I would replace the prayer book version with the gender neutral version that is based on it. I would also support including both.

2. Do we have gender neutral versions of *The Blessing of a Civil Marriage* and *An Order for Marriage*, and *A Thanksgiving for the Birth or Adoption of a Child*?

Ministration to the Sick and Ministration at the Time of Death

1. There is considerable material in our supplemental volumes. Comparisons should be made to see if any of the newer material is preferable to what is in the current BCP.

2. Healing Services have become quite popular. Should one be included? Both BOS and EOW have one.

The Burial of the Dead

1. In Rite I, I don't think the full texts of all the Psalms are necessary. They can be cited like the lessons.

2. In Rite II, the prayers that are built around biblical stories are lost on many of the people attending burial offices. They are excellent when the Lazarus gospel is used and the sermon touches on it, but otherwise I think new prayers should be composed.

3. In all the prayers that used an italicized male pronoun to indicate that the deceased could also be a woman, we need a more inclusive way to handle this. A simple *her/him* would do.

4. Should we include a note about the services for *At the Burial of a Child* or *Burial of One Who Does Not Profess the Christian Faith* in BOS 2018?

Episcopal Services

1. This is where we can make baptismal ecclesiology stand out more clearly. Like confirmation, it should be clear that this service draws from baptism.

2. A Pastoral Introduction should set the theology of ordination within the theology of baptism.

3. In either a Pastoral Introduction or Additional Directions, recommendations could be made regarding the symbolism of the rite, such as a strong baptismal symbol in the center of the platform, or very near it, so the ordination is seen as emanating from baptism.

All the *laos*, including visiting bishops, should sit together as the assembly. The platform should be used more for the symbols of the rite than for episcopal seating.

4. The Opening Rite should be the same as baptism.

5. We also should clarify consecration language and ordination language. All three rites should be referred to as ordinations. I recommend that the word "consecration" should be eliminated from the rite. For example, the header on page 520 should say "The Ordination of the Bishop" rather than "The Consecration of the Bishop."

6. The responses in the examination should be the same as in baptism. Or, more radically, we could build the examination off the Baptismal Covenant itself.

7. In The Litany for Ordinations, "For all members of your Church" should be "For all those baptized into your Church."

The Psalter

1. This is where we have to make decisions about the use of the male pronoun for God. New Zealand changed to the second person, but that raises questions regarding whether we have a translation or an adaptation of a text. Once again, if the current Psalter remains available then a more thoroughly revised adaptation can be produced.

2. I would like us to encourage the singing of Psalms by pointing to any Psalter we revise.

3. I hope we keep the thirty-day cycle of Psalms within the Psalter.

Prayers and Thanksgivings

1. As stated earlier, I see a larger integrated section of Public and Private Prayer that would include a section like this, along with the Daily Offices, Collects, Litany, and other resources that would be helpful. I would put such a section at the beginning of the book.

An Outline of the Faith

1. This is where we can include strong creation theology.

2. The first section should be titled "Creation" and set humanity within creation.

3. The theology and language used here can then be used in baptismal and eucharistic prayers.

Tables for Finding Holy Days

1. Move the Calendar from the beginning of the book to just before this section.

The Lectionary

1. Either replace with the RCL or remove and provide a description of current practice for eucharistic and daily readings. Such a description could refer to *Lesser Feasts and Fasts*, *A Great Cloud of Witnesses*, and *Weekday Eucharistic Propers*.

Appendix B

Proposals for the
Revision of the 1979 Prayer Book

Presented to Subcommittee Four of the Task Force
for Liturgical and Prayer Book Revision, July 2019

General Considerations
Kevin Moroney

1. What will be the status of the '79 prayer book?
   Clause 4 of A068 commits to "ensuring its continued use." This is an important point to consider
   at the beginning because the ongoing availability of
   the current prayer book could impact how we revise
   it. Options include:

   a. The '79 prayer book remains our official
      book but we approve alternative rites,
      including revised versions of the '79 rites
      (see clause 8 regarding "the perfection of
      rites").

b. We revise the '79 prayer book and approve a new book, honoring the desired implementation of inclusive and expansive language, creation theology, etc., but the liturgies of the '79 prayer book remain available for use.

c. We revise the '79 prayer book and understand clause 4 to mean that "continued use" means until a new prayer book is approved.

I suppose the point here is that the task force will need to define what it means to "memorialize" the '79 prayer book. I favor "b" but it's the recommendation of our subcommittee that matters.

2. How will we implement inclusive and expansive language? Clause 10 of Resolution A068 states that our liturgical revision will "utilize inclusive and expansive language and imagery for humanity and divinity." My own view on how to implement this principle will depend on how long the 1979 Rites remain available in their current form. If they will be available perpetually, I can see applying inclusive and expansive language principles throughout our revision work. If the '79 Rites will only be available until a full revision is completed, then I would suggest a more nuanced implementation of inclusive/expansive language. In Rite I, I suggest limiting our revision work in this area to language related to humanity and reducing the number of times God is referred to as "Father."

In Rite II, I would suggest building from the resolution passed at General Convention in 2018 regarding inclusive/expansive language changes in our Rite II Eucharist and strive to balance our language but keep the flow and feel of the prayers unchanged. These are pastoral considerations for those who do not seek dramatic changes to the current rites. New additions to the prayer book will be fully inclusive/expansive, building off of EOW and working with new liturgies that are produced.

3. How will we implement creation theology? Resolution A068 states that "our liturgical revision shall incorporate and express understanding, appreciation, and care of God's creation." The catechism of the prayer book could begin with a section on creation theology, rather than starting with human nature, as it now does. Also, any language in eucharistic prayers that describe us as "rulers" of creation should be removed and replaced with a more suitable word. I am not convinced that "steward" is the best word either. Collects that include themes for the four seasons could be included in the daily offices or section of prayers. Some have proposed an addition to the Baptismal Covenant.

4. And what about baptismal theology? Clause 5 states that we will "continue to engage the deep Baptismal and Eucharistic theology and practice of the 1979 Prayer Book." The prayer book was groundbreaking in how it emphasizes the centrality of baptism. With

that said, 1979 was early in the movement of what has come to be called baptismal ecclesiology, and I believe that any revision of the prayer book should include a more complete implementation of that theology. For example, the ordination rites could reflect a baptismal ecclesiology more clearly. A revision of the prayer book would also provide an opportunity to clarify the theology of baptism and how it informs a theology for confirmation. One of our new marriage rites is also built on the baptismal service.

5. Will a revised prayer book actually be a book? Clause 12 states that "our liturgical revision [will] take into consideration the use of emerging technologies." Many have noted that the cost of producing a bound volume as a new prayer book is prohibitive. We could choose to publish digitally with a smaller number of actual books. We could choose to produce a prayer book the same way we always have. A recommendation from the task force will be necessary.

6. Any full revision of the prayer book will need to consider the table of contents and issues related to formatting. For example, the '79 prayer book places the Great Vigil of Easter, Holy Baptism, and Holy Eucharist back-to-back-to-back. This makes a value statement about the centrality of the dominical sacraments and highlights the Vigil as the ultimate rite of their celebration. If one can assume that the beginning of a book is what the non-specialist will open to first, perhaps a revised prayer book could begin with

a section on "Daily Prayer for Individuals, Households, and Congregations" that could include the Daily Offices, shorter prayer offices, and a section of prayers like what we now have towards the end of the book, etc.

7. What other points of theological emphasis need to be considered but are not specifically named in the resolution? Clause 9 states that we will draw on "our Church's liturgical, cultural, racial, generational, linguistic, gender, physical ability, class and ethnic diversity in order to share common worship." Broadly speaking, I would describe the issue here as inculturation. Traditionally our prayer books reflect Anglo-European culture. How can a BCP embrace the diverse cultures of American society today?